PreDictionary

atelos

34

ISBN 987-1-891190-34-6

First edition, first printing

Cover image by Shelby Rachleff

 A t e l o s

A Project of Hips Road
Editors: Lyn Hejinian and Travis Ortiz
Design: Shelby Rachleff
Cover Design: Shelby Rachleff

MIKHAIL EPSTEIN

PreDictionary

An Exploration of Blank Spaces in Language

This book is about blank spaces in language and culture and their formative role in conceptual and artistic creativity. PreDictionary is a dictionary of would-be words that are designed to fill gaps in language and generate new concepts and meanings. Focused on the creative potential of a neologism and a dictionary entry, this book is dedicated to both poetry and poetics. The concept of lexicopoeia comes from Ralph Emerson: "Every word [lexis] was once a poem." To keep language alive, we must constantly reinvent, rejuvenate, and reanimate it – to imbue it with poetry. This means, in particular: to give birth to new words. One freshly coined word, a "lexicopoem" is the most concise genre of literature, more terse than even an aphorism. The first part of the book, "PreDictionary," includes 150 entries in 14 thematic sections. All new words are supplied with definitions and examples of usage. The second part, " ", is about blank spaces in language and culture and their formative role in major artistic movements of the 20th century. The book proposes a new sign that denotes the absence of any sign and is conveyed by quotation marks around a blank space: " ". This no-sign can be applied to many subject areas, including philosophy, theology, ethics, aesthetics, poetics, and linguistics. " " signifies, more adequately than any of these terms, the Absolute, Dao, the Endless, the Inexpressible, Différance, i.e., the ultimate condition of any signification. Each discipline has its own " ", certain "unspeakable" assumptions that need to be presented inside disciplinary frontiers, as a blank margin moved inside the medium. "   " allows language to speak the unspeakable. The third part, "A New Linguistic Turn: From Analysis to Synthesis," discusses the word- and dictionary- building process in relation to the needs of language development. The author sees the transition from the analysis to the synthesis of language as a most promising path of innovation in contemporary "post-analytic" philosophy and linguistics.

Contents

Part 3. A New Lingusitc Turn: From Analysis to Synthesis

Acknowledgments

More often than not, a dictionary is a team effort; a pre-dictionary is both less and more so. On one hand, a predictionary is a creation rather than compilation, more like a work of fiction. On the other hand, words, even individually coined, are designed to be used by many. Having a "pre-word" tested and vetted by "pre-readers" prepares it to fend for itself. I was fortunate to have many gifted and insightful readers for this collection who advised me on various aspects of this dangerous enterprise. Unlike a traditional lexicographer, collector of words, the "harmless drudge" (to use Dr. Samuel Johnson's definition), the inventor of words often looks like an *insolent dissenter* who defies Tradition and usurps the Public's prerogative of shaping the Language.

This book would never have reached fruition without the support of my friend Lyn Hejinian, an outstanding poet, essayist and avant-garde thinker who encouraged me to publish this lexicopoetic collection. Lyn was the organizer and the soul of the conference "Medium & Margin: Multiplying Methodologies & Proliferating Poetics" at Berkeley where I presented an experimental paper on "   " now comprising the second part of this little book. Lyn's enthusiasm and inspiration have been formative for this project, and my first gratitude goes to her.

The late Eve Adler, a wonderful friend and magnificent translator of one of my books, was the invaluable reader and advisor on the initial, short 2002 version of *Predictionary*. She suggested the name *lexicopoeia* for the genre I initially called *lexipoeia*. Dmitry Shalin, another good friend and sociology professor (University of Nevada), read my early drafts with a constructive skepticism and provided generous advice, which I have followed to the end. I discussed intermediate drafts with Mary Cappello, a talented essayist (University of Rhode Island), and some entries with my long-standing friend Gene Barabtarlo, a literary scholar (University of Missouri), and benefited a lot from their refined advice. The brilliant translator of another book of mine, Dr. Anesa Miller has carefully edited the *Predictionary* when it was still significantly shorter than now, and added stylistic elegance to numerous examples. Igor Klyukanov from East Washington University has accurately yet inventively translated from Russian " " and "Semiurgy" parts and edited the Introduction and some of the later entries. Every of the several versions of the book invited new editing; the last one was edited by Vassili Belov of Maplewood, NJ, with whom I was also lucky to discuss some coinages and their possible implications. Without these friends and colleagues, their professional expertise, linguistic taste and generous moral support, this book would very different or non-existent at all.

Every word was once
a poem…

Ralph Emerson

…as is every emerging word.

Preface

Dictionaries, even those that accommodate neologisms, tend to be reactive, i.e., reflect what has already happened with the language. A **predictionary**, on the other hand, is proactive as it contributes new words that may make their way into the language and dictionaries of the future.

The term "predictionary" can be read two ways:
(1) pre-dictionary: a draft, a beginning, a prototype of a dictionary;
(2) prediction-ary: a collection of predictions, of would-be words or words to-be, of vocabulary hopefuls.

Both readings are correct, even necessary to understand what predictionary is all about: predicting and introducing new words (rather than recording those already in use) to be potentially included over time into regular dictionaries.

This Predictionary is a collection of words that I have coined since the early 1980s. The project has three objectives: analytic, aesthetic, and pragmatic.

1. Analytically, the Predictionary looks for gaps and semantic voids in the lexical and conceptual system of the language in order to fill them with new words describing potential things and emerging ideas.

2. Aesthetically, the Predictionary aims to create miniature works of verbal art, micropoems, lexipoems. Filled with drama and intrigue, these novel pieces of language open new avenues for thought and imagination by provocatively juxtaposing available word-forming elements.

3. Pragmatically, the Predictionary seeks to introduce new words into the language by providing examples of their usage. Each word is defined and illustrated to show its communicative value and the range of possible applications in typical situations and contexts.

It is my hope that most of these suggested words will achieve the first goal, and at least some will approach the second; the third may prove unattainable, yet hope again prevails over experience. As Fyodor Tyutchev, 19th century Russian poet, put it:

It is beyond our power to fathom
Which way the word we utter resonates,
Thus, like a sudden grace that comes upon us,
A gift of empathetic understanding emanates.

Introduction.
Lexicopoeia
as a Literary Genre

What is the minimal genre, the elementary unit of literary creativity? Not an aphorism or a maxim, as many would immediately suggest. The unit of verbal creativity is a neologism — a single word as a "quantum" of creative energy. A new word reveals in the most concentrated form the same qualities of invention as longer literary texts, such as a poem or a novel.

This unit of creative verbal output can be called **verbit**, blending *verbal* and *bit*; the shared *b* joining them into a single word. An example of a **verbit** is the word *verbit* itself.

Various types of neologisms perform various linguistic and social functions: technical terms, trademarks and brand names, political slogans, expressive coinages in literature and journalism... Authors like Lewis Carrol or James Joyce wove neologisms into the fabric of their writing. However, a neologism should be recognized as a self-sufficient text. I call this genre of producing single words **lexicopoeia**, from the Greek *lexis*, 'word' (from *legein*, 'say') and *poiein*, 'to make or create'. Lexicopoeia means word-composition, word-formation. It is a literary genre of its own, the poetry of a single word.

Ralph Emerson's phrase chosen as the epigraph is a good definition of lexicopoeia:

Every word [lexis] was once a poem [poiema]

To which I would add "…as **is** every emerging word." As we get too accustomed to words, use them routinely, our speech tends to become dull and flavorless. To keep language alive, we must constantly reinvent, rejuvenate, and reanimate it, to imbue it with poetry. This means, in particular: to give birth to new words.

Lexicopoeia is the most concise genre of literature. Even aphorisms seem cumbersome and verbose compared with a **lexicopoem**. The genre of aphorism deals with sentences, while the lexicopoem focuses on the word as the smallest meaningful unit of language fit for independent use.

Roots, prefixes, suffixes and other word-building blocks (morphemes) provide the material for lexicopoeia. Not any combination of morphemes would make a new word, just as not any combination of words would make an aphorism, a poem or a story. A lexicopoem is the atomary text with its own idea, imagery, composition, plot, and relations/references to other words. That's what makes lexicopoeia an art rather than random morpheme-blending. The meaning of a lexicopoem cannot be mechanically derived from the separate meanings of its morphological components.

The word "lexicopoeia" is an example of the very genre it designates; it is also a fresh coinage never used before in English or any other language; you won't find it in any dictionary or web source.

The preceding sentence was written in 2003 when I first put my collection online on my web page at Emory University. By June 2011, searching for "lexicopoeia" would yield 673 web pages. Among other words I first posted on various websites in 2003, searching for "predictionary" now yields 10,500 pages; for "protologism," 10,300; "lovedom," 13,100; "cerebrity," 45,600; "syntellect," 140,000; and "dunch," 414,000 pages.[1] The words "sovok" (Homo Sovieticus) and "metarealism" (an artistic and literary movement) that I introduced into Russian in the 1980s, have migrated into English and now yield 1,430,000 and 30,000 web pages, respectively. Words, like books, have their own fate. The Web is a perfect tool to track down word origins and spread.

In the process of putting together this lexicopoetic collection I initially checked all my coinages on Google to make sure none has been used before, at least in the meaning proposed in this book.[2] Of course, I make no claim to be the first and only person to have introduced these words. It's not unusual for several minds to come up with the same new word independently. As Alan Metcalf puts it, "[n]ot only are words easily born, they are also easily reborn. The majority of new words that endure are coined not just once, but many times before they become

1. From 2003 I contributed my coinages to several websites open to such free submissions: Urban Dictionary; Merriam-Webster Open Dictionary; Wictionary; Pseudodictionary; Unwords Dictionary; Peripatetic forums (Neologisms); Dictionary.com Forum; English Discussion Forums — UsingEnglish.com; Google news groups, such as alt.english.usage, alt.usage.english, sci.lang, and others. I attempted to sow the seeds of new words as widely as possible, in hope that they may give rise to new ways of expression and conceptualization.
2. To look for my first online publications of any given word, you can search it on Google in conjunction with my name and surname.

established…. Just as the calculus was independently invented by both Newton and Leibniz when mathematics was ready for it, so new words appear again and again when the language is ready."[3]

It is hard to describe what it takes to coin a new word and at which point we can consider it born. When it dawns upon one's mind? Has been uttered? written down? defined? used in a phrase? used consistently in private conversations and public discussions? When it catches public attention? becomes so convincing and emotionally charged that people are increasingly tempted to use it?

So a newborn word goes through a number of lifecycle stages. Though the word itself may have occurred spontaneously and simultaneously to many minds, it does matter who takes care of it, tries to "civilize" it, to provide definitions, contexts, interpretations and convincing examples of usage. Parenting does not stop at birth, it takes persistent efforts nurturing, culturing, and educating the newborn, providing it with means of subsistence and introducing it to society. Fortunately, the Web, for the first time in human history, offers a tremendous opportunity for researching the origins and destinies of new words, at least those that have emerged during the age of electronics.

---

3. Allan Metcalf. *Predicting New Words: The Secrets of Their Success*. Boston, New York: Houghton Mifflin Company, 2002. p. 97.

Protologisms vs. Neologisms

The genre of PreDictionary, however eccentric or even egocentric it may seem, has a long tradition in English. In 1531, Sir Thomas Elyot in *The Boke called the Gouernor*, the earliest treatise on moral philosophy in English, set the task of purposely extending the national vocabulary by introducing new words. "I intended to augment our Englyshe tongue wherby men shulde as well expresse more abundantly the thynge that they Conceyued in their hartis (wherfore language was ordeyned)…" His neologisms include many masterpieces that were to become staples of the English language, such as *activity, audacity, education, exactly, involve, mediocrity, sincerity,* and *society.*

It is hard to imagine that nowadays one can emulate the linguistic feat of Sir Thomas Elyot and his abundant gifts to the English language. As a language matures, it tends to become less malleable. But even a single word successfully introduced into common usage can bring its inventor recognition like a famous poem to its author. Such is the case of the humorist-writer and illustrator Gelett Burgess whose best known legacy is the word *blurb* published in *Burgess Unabridged: A New Dictionary of Words You Have Always Needed* (1914). Out of a hundred words offered in this edition only one took hold and persisted. Then, what would we call the rest of Burgess's words that evidently had their own conceptual and poetic value, such as *edicle* ("one who is educated beyond his intellect") or *gubble* ("society talk, the hum of foolish conversation")? They had never achieved the status of neologisms, i.e. words more or less adopted by the language though still perceived as newcomers (*blog* and *truthiness* are recent examples).

I suggest calling such brand new words "**protologisms**" (Gr *protos*, first, original + Gr *logos*, word; cf. *prototype*, *protoplasm*). Protologism is a freshly minted and not yet widely accepted word. It is a prototype, a pilot lexical unit which may eventually be adopted for a public service or remain a whim of linguo-poetic imagination. Protologisms and neologisms are different age groups of verbal population. Along with the decrepit, obsolescent archaisms facing death, and strong, thriving middle-aged words that make up the bulk of the vocabulary, we should recognize neologisms (youngsters vigorously making their way into public spaces) and protologisms (newborns still in their cradles and nurtured by their parents). Once a protologism has found its way into media, it becomes a neologism. Every newly coined word, even if deliberately promoted for general or commercial use, has initially been a protologism; none can skip that infancy phase. As it achieves public recognition, it gets upgraded to neologism; once firmly established in public domain, it becomes "just a word."

Over the last few years some words I proposed, e.g., "dunch" or "lovedom," have been gradually turning from protologisms into neologisms, with tens of thousands of web hits. But the majority of words found in this book are still babies, protologisms, and the word "protologism" is one of them... Or is it? With 10,000 webpages showing it on Google, can we count it as a neologism? Neologisms are hard to tell from protologisms based on numbers alone. How many leaves it takes to get a "heap"? Ten, twenty, a hundred, a thousand? It is a matter of convention. I would suggest considering any word used independently by at least ten authors and found on at least a thousand webpages a neologism.

A protologism, however, doesn't have to strive ambitiously to become a neologism; childhood has its own charm and value. Kids are blessed with imagination and creativity that often fade as people mature. Sometimes a poetic word – a "one-word poem" – may be deemed unfit for practical purposes precisely because of its poetic nature. It may be a good poem or a bad poem, but it has to be judged in aesthetic rather than functional terms. Lexicopoeia as an art judges the words based on such essential criteria as wit, power of imagination, expressive and inventive energy, conceptual courage rather than potential for general circulation and routine usage. It is the imaginative quality of protologisms rather than the practical usefulness of neologisms that this collection attempts to celebrate. Fortunately, one does not necessarily exclude the other.

* * *

The first part of the book includes one hundred fifty entries (protologisms) divided into fourteen thematic sections. Within each section, the order of entries is alphabetic, with several exceptions for cognate words that cluster together.

Then, as verbal signs run out, a nonverbal one – in fact, a no-sign – emerges: "   ", inherently unpronounceable and unverbalizable. The second part, riddled with white holes, imitates Power Point format, with short statements on separate "slides" leaving ample room to emphasize the "   " as the environment that surrounds the text and fills it with gaps.

The third part discusses the word- and dictionary-generating process (the semiurgy, or sign-producing) in relation to the needs of language development and the web potential. Finally, I focus on the dictionary entry as a synthetic genre which even better reflects the purposes of this project than the genre of a single word, emphasized in the Introduction.

PreDictionary

Everyday Life

dunch *n* (a portmanteau of *lunch* and *dinner*; cf. *brunch*) — a snack between lunch and dinner in the late afternoon or early evening.

Dunch better describes the midway meal than the once suggested "linner." Dunch is a lighter meal, more similar to lunch than to dinner. Accordingly, the word is shorter and follows the pattern of the recently coined "brunch." Our urban life, with its proliferating social occasions and meetings over meals, may make this term handy.

> **Dunch** usually includes tea or coffee with cookies, sometimes fruits or a salad.

> I already have plans for lunch and dinner tomorrow; let's have a **dunch**.

etceteric *adj* (from *etcetera*) — mentioned under "etc." among many other items, not worthy to be named individually; generic, anonymous, unimportant.

> Alan has worked in this field for almost forty years, and he's still an **etceteric** researcher. Isn't that a shame?

> Kaluga is not an **etceteric** Russian town, it is famous for the best preserved 19th century cityscape.

I'm afraid you've never heard of Andrew Lynch. No, he is not an esoteric writer. He is simply an **etceteric** writer.

eventify *v trans* — to make more eventful, to spice up.

Do you want to **eventify** your life? To make it fuller, more exciting? Come travel with us.

Let's think how we could **eventify** our next vacation.

Our relationship is becoming a routine. I'm looking for ways to **eventify** it.

Eventifying your life may seem like a good idea, but might actually prove destructive.

orgy of order — a meaningless order imposed by an outside force.

My wife organized the papers on my desk. They were a mess alright, but I knew perfectly well which was where. I came back and found an **orgy of order**: neat but meaningless stacks of papers.

traf *v* (back-formation from *traffic*) — to drive in heavy, slow traffic, to be stuck in traffic.

(Back-formation is the creation of a simpler, shorter form of a longer word, like "edit" from "editor," "intuit" from "intuition.")

I **traffed** for an hour before I got home.

veery *adj* (blend of *very* and *veer*) — an emphatic, emotional form of "very"; to the highest degree, in the fullest sense possible. Also associated with "to veer" (from Lat *vibrare*, vibrate) and, accordingly, implies "making a huge difference," "extreme," "crucial," "ultimate."

Thank you **veery** much!

This is a **veery** important paper.

Veery truly yours.

People and Characters

chairy *adj* — someone who likes to chair meetings, to preside, to be a master of ceremonies.

> Jimmy is every bit as **chairy** as Andrew, which spells trouble for a small institution like ours.

> She is a wonderful person, but perhaps a touch too **chairy** to make a pleasant housemate.

doctator *n* (*doctor* + *dictator*) — doctor as dictator, an agent of medical tyranny.

doctatorship *n* — the dictatorship of doctors; the system of medical coercion with mandatory treatments enforced by hospitals and insurance companies. Pressure from health officials leaves the patient no choice.

> They insist on this course of treatment because it's profitable for the clinic. **Doctatorship** is a grave danger to society.

domestican *n* — someone who preaches the values of domestic life, hearth and home.

> A typical **domestican** hates going outside and prefers kitchen and living room to all attractions of the world.

He is as reclusive as a monk, though his monastery is his own house. In a word, he is a **domestican**.

fatenik *n* (*fate* + suffix *-nik*) — someone who flirts with the idea of fate, constantly watches for omens, checks horoscopes, etc.

-nik is a Russian suffix that made its way into English in 1957 with *sputnik* (cf. similarly derived *beatnik*, *peacenik*, *refusenik*, etc.) and usually refers to persons with a certain inclination or bias.

A fatalist believes that everything is predetermined and inevitable. A **fatenik** is a playful and superficial fatalist who enjoys signs of the supernatural without giving them much importance.

> Never mind Lisa's premonitions. She is a **fatenik** and easily picks up stupid rumors.

ifnik *n* (*if* + suffix *nik*) — someone whose life, habits and thinking are shaped by countless "ifs" rather than hu's own will or convictions.[4]

> Don't ask him what he's going to do. A typical **ifnik**, he will give you a dozen of "ifs."

---

4. Hu pron (a clipping of "human") — a 3rd person gender-neutral pronoun referring both to a man and a woman — pronounced (hju:), like "hu" in "human." Hu suggests the meaning of undivided humanness. "Hu's" stands for "his or her." More information on this pronoun is given in the last section "Grammati-cal Words."

meetnik *n* (*meet* + suffix *nik*) — a person who eagerly attends and enjoys any business meetings.

> Being social is one thing, meeting for the sake of meeting is another. I try to stay away from **meetniks** for whom getting together is an end in itself.

safenik *n* (*safe* + suffix *nik*) — a person who wants everything warranted, feels an overwhelming need for safety and security and is scared by the vicissitudes of life.

> How about a family trip to Tibet? — No way. My husband is a safenik, he never takes any risks.

whynik *n* (*why* + suffix *nik*) — a person too eager to know why things are the way they are and pestering everybody with questions.

The association with *whiner* and *whimper* makes this word even more expressive describing children who often are both whyniks and whiners.

> This little **whynik** drives me mad. Make him stop asking.

Emotions and Psychology

astralgia *n* (Gr *astro-*, star + Gr *algos* — pain, grief, distress; cf. *nostalgia*) — a longing for stars and space travel to remote corners of the universe; being homesick for the cosmos.

> *Gattaca* (the film) is about **astralgia**. The main character, deemed genetically flawed and thus given an unskilled job, pursues his dream of space travel.

avidominosis *n* (Lat *videre*, to see; *avitaminosis*, vitamins deficiency) — the shortage of visual impressions, craving to see new landscapes, films, spectacles, works of art, etc.

> I feel an urge to go to the cinema. Because of my home bound lifestyle and months of non-stop reading and writing I've developed an acute **avidominosis**.

conaster *n* (Lat *cum*, with + Gr *astron*, star) — literally *with* star, the antonym to *disaster* (literally "away from stars"); the fortunate outcome of an imminent disaster; the sensation of a dodged catastrophe remembered from the vantage point of safety.

> There were several **conasters** in my life that I can only attribute to God's undeserved mercy.

> You were born under a lucky star. This **conaster** was an amazing mix of chance and miracle.

conastrous *adj* — of the nature of a conaster, causing great relief.

> I had a **conastrous** experience after being caught in a storm while windsurfing.

egonautics *n* (Lat *ego*, I + Gr *nautikos*, of ships and sailing, cf. *aeronautics*, *astronautics*) — adventurous exploration of one's self.

egonaut *n* — a person dedicated to navigating one's self.

> **Egonauts** are adventurous intraverts who travel to the frontiers of their mind and body to discover new lands.

> John is constantly experimenting on himself. **Egonautics** is his passion.,

experimence *n* (*experience* + *experiment*) — experience based on experiments, or an experiment based on experience.

Both *experience* and *experiment* come from the Latin *experiri*, to try or test; the two meanings have split in English in the 14th century but still have much in common. **Experimence** comes handy where one want both meanings combined.

> My **experimences** with love have been more desperate than daring.

> Ivan Karamazov's **experimence** in rejecting God results in madness.

happicle *n* (*happy* + suffix *-icle*, as in *particle*, *icicle*) — a single happy occurrence or a momentary feeling of happiness, a particle of happiness.

> **Happicles** make life worth living, even a not too happy one.

> There is no happiness in this world, but there are **happicles**. Sometimes we can catch them, fleeting and unpredictable as they are.

> **Happicles**, like photons, have zero mass at rest — they lack the stable nature that defines happiness. **Happicles** flash and go, ephemeral as a fragrance, a falling leaf, or a passerby's glance.

multividual *n* (Lat *multus*, many + Lat *individuus*, indivisible) — a multiple-personality individual with many selves.

> Psychologists have noticed the emergence of a protean type of personality combin-ing properties of different individuals: not a schizophrenically split personality, but a healthy **multividual** who cannot be confined to a single self.

> In the past, **multividuals** often revealed their multiple selves in acts of artistic in-spiration and creative reincarnation. With the progress of technology, these multiple selves may acquire independent bodies and reach across continents under various physical guises performing vari-ous social and professional roles.

narrow(ly) awake — mostly asleep, doz-ing; the opposite of "wide awake."

I haven't slept all night, so don't expect me to be coherent; I am **narrowly awake**.

oneirogenic *adj* (from Gr *oneiros*, dream + *genic*; cf. *photogenic*, *telegenic*) — having a propensity to appear in somebody's dreams.

Some people are photogenic, others, **oneirogenic**; these abilities rarely coincide. Someone hardly noticeable in real life may haunt our dreams and imagination.

Have you noticed that cats are more **oneirogenic** than dogs?

Ask your friends, "Do you find me "**oneirogenic**"? If the answer is "yes," ask them to recall what were your actions in their dreams.

transvert *n* (Lat *trans*, across, over + *vertere*, to turn; cf. *introvert*, *extrovert*) — a psychological type switching between introversion and extroversion and combin-ing features of both types.

I'm neither an extravert or an introvert; a **transvert**, I would say. My ways defy classification.

His life switches between extremes of self-absorbed seclusion and wild partying at random places with random people. He is a typical **transvert**.

Relationships and Communication

ambipathy *n* (Gr *amphi-* or Lat *ambi-*, both, on both sides + Gr *pathos*, feeling) — a mixture of sympathy and antipathy, attraction and repulsion; a condition of being torn apart by conflicting feelings and aspi-rations.

> Catullus's phrase "I hate and love" is an early expression of **ambipathy**.

> Dostoevsky's characters often prove **ambipathic** as they alienate and torture those whom they love.

defriend *v trans* (*de* + *friend*; cf. *befriend*) — to break off friendly relations.

> He **defriended** me a year after we met, for no reason. He just stopped calling, pe-riod.

> I want to **defriend** you. —What's wrong? —I need more than friendship from you. I need love.

goodevil *n* (*good* + *evil*) - the intended good that, if implemented consistently and with violence, turns into evil, with the devil as a mediator.

> Grand Inquisitor in Dostoevsky exemplifies **goodevil**: the good that is enforced on people destroys them.

goodevilish *adj*

> "With an iron hand we'll drive the humanity to happiness," –
> this was a a **goodevilish** slogan of Rusian revolution.

hi-byer *n* (*hi* + *bye* + suffix -*er*) — a mar-ginal acquaintance,
with verbal exchange limited mostly to "hi" and "bye".

> Do you know her? — Not really, we are **hi-byers**.

> I was surprised to see this **hi-byer** stop-ping for a substantial
> conversation.

> They were married for ten years, but now they are simply
> **hi-byers**.

mehemize *v* (from *mhm* — a sound whereby a listener con-
firms hearing, with-out agreeing or disagreeing) — to confirm
listening and understanding with no defini-tive response to what
is being said.

> Empathetic **mehemizing** is a token of diplomatic
> conversation.

mehemic *adj* — related to the mhm sound (see above).

> What was his reaction to your proposal? — **Mehemic.**
> Neither yes nor no.

mutually mute — verbally incompatible persons.

Some people feel awkward of silence and try to say something though they have nothing to say to each other.

> I respect Dr. Stone but we are **mutually mute**. When we meet, we squeeze out some nonsense about weather and sports in which neither of us has the slightest in-terest.

Life, Health and Death

biogram *n* (Gr *bio*, life + Gr *gram*, letter) — a section of life experience, a building block of biography.
Biograms include "love," "friendship," "marriage," "travel," "illness," "war," etc., i.e. any event(s) perceived as a structural unit of life narrative.

> A traditional biography presents **biograms** chronologically, whereas a biographic dictionary of an outstanding personality would present the biograms in systematic order: areas of work, achievements, ideas, publications, awards, friends, co-workers, places, major personal and historical events, etc.

bioplagiarism *n* — unsolicited or illegitimate cloning.

> **Bioplagiarism** is a violation of each human's copyright to the unique text of hu's body.

> Any organism is a book of unmarked quotations from its ancestors. **Bioplagiarism** is in the order of things.

sanitas insania (Lat *sanitas*, health + Lat *insania*, mania) — obsession with health and wellness.
Sanitas insania is an oxymoron. To be obsessed with health is unhealthy.

> Steve washes his hands every five minutes in fear of infection – a typical symptom of **sanitas insania**.

smort *n* (*sport* + *mort*, mortal) — self-ruinous obsession with sport; health-damaging stress and exhaustion from physical exercise.

smortive *adj* — obsessed with physical exercise and fitness to the detriment of health.

smortsman, smortswoman *n* — a smortive person.

> This **smortive** guy is jogging for four hours now, running to meet his early death.

> Please don't let your love of fitness turn you into a **smortsman**.

thanatagogy *n* (Gr *thanatos*, death + Gr *agein*, to lead; cf. *pedagogy*, *demagogy*) — initiation into death, preparation for dying.

> **Thanatology** is theoretical study of death; thanatogogy is a practical discipline, a pedagogy of dying.

> The Egyptian "Book of the Dead" is the earliest handbook of **thanatagogy**.

> Plato sees philosophy as the basis of **thanatagogy**: to study philosophy means preparing oneself to die.

thanatagog or **thanatagogue** *n* — a person who leads into death, prepares old or terminally ill people for dying.

> He is a **thanatagog** by vocation. He works at a hospice.

Love and Sex

amoresque *n* (cf. *humoresque, arabesque*) — a short literary or musical piece on love, often with whimsical or fantastic motifs.

> He wants to write a new Decameron, a collection of **amoresques** about men and women of any imaginable orientation.

amorist *n* (from Lat. *amor*, love; cf. *humorist*) — an author who specializes in ro-mance novels; an expert in love and mar-riage; someone preoccupied with or experi-enced in love and eroti-cism.

> Danielle Steele is a famous **amorist**, author of dozens of sentimental novels for women.

> He switched from landscape painting to love scenes and now he is mostly an **amorist**.

> If you want good advice on your affair, ask John. He is an experienced **amorist**.

amoristic *adj* — dealing with love or eros as a matter of verbal or visual discourse (cf. *amorous*, related to love itself)

> *Sex and the City*? Sorry, I don't share your **amoristic** interests. I'd rather see a historic movie.

amorism *n* (cf. *aphorism*) — a concise statement, popular saying or general wis-dom on love.

> Steve certainly has a great deal of experience with women, but his **amorisms** are trite and superficial.

amort *n* (Lat *amor*, love + Lat *mors*, death) — the mixed love/death instinct; the union of Eros and Thanatos, or trans-forma-tion of one into another; a cruel passion destroying the loved and/or the lover.

> **Amort** is the most common theme of Eu-ropean literature, from *Tristan and Isolde* to Oscar Wilde's *The Ballad of Reading Gaol* ("And all men kill the thing they love…")

amortify *v trans.* (Lat *amor*, love + *mortify*) — to act with both affection and ruth-lessness, to inflict suffering and ruin by love.

> Dostoevsky's novel *The Idiot* is about people who keep trying to **amortify** each other — and eventually succeed.

armand *n* (from *Armand*, proper name) — an adolescent boy with a sexual cha-risma, a male counterpart to Nabokov's nymphet. In Thomas Mann's novel *The Confessions of Felix Krull, Confidence Man*,[5] a mature woman (a counterpart of Nabokov's Humbert Humbert) calls Felix, her teenage lover, **Armand** (pos-sibly associated with Fr *amant*, lover), and says "I detest the

---

5. Thomas Mann. *The Confessions of Felix Krull, Confidence Man.* New York, Alfred Knopf, 1955, p. 176.

grown man full-bearded and wooly-chested... It's only you boys I have loved from the beginning... ."

> In *Lolita*, Nabokov uses the phrase "a little Faun" to describe a nymphet's male counterpart. Essentially, *nymphet*, *Lolita*, *little Faun*, and **armand** all describe a heterosexual attraction of adults to young teenagers.

> The school teacher looked for **armands** among her students – and found one. By the time he turned fourteen she was pregnant by him.

bangover *n* (*bang* + *over*; cf. *hangover*) — exhaustion and other after-effects of sexual indulgence or arousal.

> You are looking kinda haggard, my friend. A hangover? — Well, and **bangover**, too.

> The Japanese have a word derived from "sex-over," "sekusu oba." Vials of special pick-me-up are sold to morning commuters at rail stations. In English, we could call it **bangover**, or **sexhaustion**.

dislove *v trans* (prefix *dis-* + *love*) — to have a deep negative feeling, attraction-through-aversion to somebody.

"**Dislove**" is a deeper feeling than "dislike," a matter of personal relationship rather than taste. **Disloving** implies a strong negative emotional connection to its hu-man object.

> I **dislove** my ex-husband, I don't dislike him. I would never marry someone I simply dislike.

equiphilia *n* (Gr *aequi*, equal + *philia*, love) — indiscriminate love of many per-sons or things.

> **Equiphilia** may be close to indifference. Equal love to many means no love at all.

> Mary has hard time making up her mind. Not that she is indifferent to her admirers but she is now at the point of **equiphilia**.

eroticon *n* — a lexicon of love: thoughts, stories, speech fig-ures related to love, eros, and romance.

> Roland Barthes' *A Lover's Discourse* is an outstanding example of **eroticon**.

lovedom *n* (*love* + suffix -*dom*) — the world of love, the totality of loving emotions and relationships.

> Edward VIII was that rare romantic who challenged society by trading his kingdom for **lovedom**.

> Your heart is large enough to love many, but can you find a small corner for me in your **lovedom**?

philocracy (Gr *philos*, loving + *kratos*, power, rule) — the rule of love; love as a governing principle of social and commu-nal life.

philocrat — a believer in the power of love, in love-based governance.

Philocracy assumes that God, who is Love, is the source of all authority. Hence, love should be the ultimate authority.

Philocracy is different from theocracy that implies the power of organized relig-ion and would be better termed *hierocracy* — government by the clergy, ecclesiastical rule.

philophilia *n* (Gr *philia*, love) — love for love's sake.

Todd is a **philophil**. He does not love anybody in particular, he just enjoys be-ing in love.

philophobia *n* (Gr *philia*, love + *phobia*, fear) — a fear of love and intimacy.

Stalin had **philophobia**: he never had a deep personal relationship with anybody, like friendship or love.

retrosexual *n* (Lat *retro*, backward + *sexual*; cf. *metrosexual*) — a person of main-stream sexuality, sexual conservative.

Mathew has never even tried oral sex, he is a **retrosexual**.

sexhaustion *n* (*sex* + *exhaustion*) — same as bangover.

siamorous *adj* (*Siamese* + *amorous*) — closely connected by a psychic symbiosis based on love.

Do you see this **siamorous** couple? They live next door for 20 years, and I've never seen them walking separately.

– Your boyfriend was flirting with that redhead. – It's OK, we're not **siamorous**, I've been flirting with Bob, too.

spectrosexual *n* (*specter* + *sexual*) — someone looking for an ideal, illusive and elusive sexual partner.

> Some see Don Juan not as erotomaniac but as a **spectrosexual** who loved the idea of the female more than real women.

womaneuver *n* or *v* (*woman* + *maneuver*) - to act in a female manner, to use feminine tactics for achieving one's goals.

> **Womaneuvering** is a strategy to convert your weaknesses into advantages.

> He tried to outmaneuver her but was helpless against **womaneuvering**.

Mind and Knowledge

cerebrity *n* (Lat *cerebrum*, brain; cf. *celebrity*) — a famous intellectual; a cerebral but emotionally dry or egocentric person.

> I avoid meetings with **cerebrities**. Everything they have to say is already in their books.

> I used to think of Hegel as a **cerebrity** with little human passions, and was surprised to learn that he fathered an illegitimate son.

gnawledge *n* (portmanteau of *gnaw* and *knowledge*) — mechanical knowledge obtained by "gnawing" facts rather than by conceptualizing and creatively interpreting them.
Gnawledge and *knowledge* are homophones (differ only in spelling).

> When Bacon said "knowledge is power," he didn't meant **gnawledge**.

inventure *n* (*invention* + *adventure*) — a creative and engaging intellectual undertaking.

> This book about the invention of radio reads like a thriller, with one **inventure** upon another.

> By cutting reason down to size and establishing its "proper"

limits, Kant encouraged subsequent **inventures**, a never-ending quest to reach beyond the limits of rational thought.

inventurer *n* — an adventurer in the world of ideas and inventions.

> **Inventurers** know how much there is that they don't know and start their journey confessing their ignorance, like Socrates or Kant.

noocracy *n* (Gr *noos*, mind + Gr -*kratia*, power or rule) — the rule of mind, a system of world government based on the civilization's consolidated intelligence.

> The future of humanity can be envisioned as **noocracy** — the power of the collective brain representing certain social groups or society as whole, rather than individuals.

Paleonoic *adj* (Gr *palaios*, ancient + Gr *noos*, mind; cf. *Paleozoic* era, from Gr *zoe*, life) — the current epoch of primitive mind and first intelligent machines; in the future history of consciousness this era will occupy a place similar to that of the Paleozoic in the history of life.

> From the perspective of a distant future, we are people of the **Paleonoic** era, when the first non-biological forms of reason were just emerging, when thinking left at last the prison of the brain with the emergence of computers and other forms of artificial intelligence.

syntellect *n* (Gr *syn*, with, together + *intellect*) — the consolidated mind of civilization that integrates all individual minds, both natural and artificial, through information networks.

> InteLnet, the intellectual network, will connect all thinking beings into one network that will evolve over time into a new form of consciousness — **syntellect**. The **syntellect** will consolidate all the thinking potential of civilization and operate on both biological and quantum levels.

Philosophy

beable *n, adj* (*to be* + suffix *able*) — having a potential for being.

> What is thinkable and imaginable in our world is also **beable** in one of the possible worlds.

> A fetus is not a being yet, it is just a **beable**.

bject *n* (common part of *subject* and *object*) — one that is both a subject and object, i.e. in an undetermined position, or superposition, of being the actor and the acted upon. It is a more fundamental category than "subject" or "object."

> When we say that "the sea is seething," the sea is a "**bject**," i.e. both the subject and object of seething.

fantology *n* (*fantasy* + -*ology*) — a study of possible worlds and fantastic beings bridging philosophical thought and artistic imagination.

> The task of **fantology** is to explore potentialities of being, including those of alternative worlds.

nove *n* (from Lat *novus*, new) — a unit of newness or novelty, something new, unexpected, unusual.

A bit is a unit of *information* obtained by learning which of the two equally likely events occurred. A **nove** is a unit of *creativity* obtained by finding which of many equally improbable ideas is most provable, viable and feasible.

> How many **noves** have you identified in this artistic project?

reity *n* (Lat *re*, matter or thing) — all that is real in opposition to the virtual.

Reity is narrower than "reality." Virtual worlds are parts of a larger reality that embraces abstract concepts, emotional states, numbers, fantasies, etc. **Reity** is what we find around ourselves when we turn off our computers and leave the virtual worlds: the aroma of coffee, the sound of a living voice, a view from the window...

> Switching to **reity** from a video or a computer is a gratifying experience. You sense afresh the charm of things as they smell and taste and touch you.

sophiophilia *n* (Gr *sophia*, wisdom + *philia*, love; cf. *philosophy*) — love for wisdom that cannot be reduced to any academic discipline or discourse, including philosophy.

> Over the last two millennia philosophy has variously defined itself as a rational theology, a universal science, an ideology, a method of analyzing language, but seldom as **sophiophilia**, i.e. the love for wisdom proper.

sophiophil *n* — someone who loves wisdom in a non-philosophical way.

Philosophy has strayed so far from wisdom that love for wisdom needs a different name. One can be a **sophiophil** without taking any interest in today's academic philosophy.

scientify *v trans* (*science* + suffix *-ify*, from Lat *-ficare* or *-facere*, to make or do) — to make something more scientific, subject to scientific analysis, rules and concepts.

He tried hard to **scientify** his paper, but it is still a provocative essay rather than a consistent argument.

She **scientified** her diet and as a result lost her appetite.

white holes *n* — cultural gaps among signs and symbols that point out a need for new words and concepts (cf. *black holes* in the outer space).

White holes, as defined in physics, throw out matter and energy, in contrast to black holes that swallow things irretrievably. Physics argues that white holes cannot exist, since that would violate the second law of thermodynamics. The laws of physics, however, do not apply to culture, noosphere and semiosphere, where **white holes** do exist. One of the goals of the humanities is to extract energy from such semantic voids, **white holes**, and fill them with new signs and ideas.

Religion and Beliefs

esoterra *n* (*esoteric*, occult + Lat *terra*, land) — an enchanted country, a mysterious or miraculous land.

> India, with her myriads of deities, is a quintessential **esoterra**.

ghostalgia *n* (*ghost* + Gr *algos* — pain, grief, distress; cf. *nostalgia*) — a mystical longing or wistful affection for ghosts, angels, aliens, and other paranormal and mysterious phenomena.

> **Ghostalgia** is a form of nostalgia for the other world as our true lost home.

> I am agnostic, but sometimes feel **ghostalgic**.

> In times of crisis, **ghostalgia** can grip the souls of entire nations.

relicious *adj* (*relic* + *religious*) — religiously devoted to relics, to the preservation of the past.

> Nothing in modern life is meaningful to him. He is a deeply **relicious** person, not simply nostalgic.

> To some people Eastern Orthodox spirituality seems more **relicious** than truly religious.

Slavior *n* (to (en)*slave* + suffix *ior*, like in *savior*) — the prince of this world, the Antichrist, who claims to be the savior but enslaves people pretending to save them.

> For those eschatologically-minded, the distinction between Savior and **Slavior** may be as subtle as one letter difference in their names.

> Some Christians believe that the **Slavior** is already here, in our very midst, and refuse to serve this impostor.

theomonism *n* (from Gr *theos*, God + Gr *monos*, one) — unity in God; the integration of various religious traditions and denominations achieved through common faith in one God, in the oneness of God. **Theomonism** is the reversal and eventual historical outcome of *monotheism*.

> There are three major stages in the religious history of mankind. Many gods — many faiths: polytheism, such as the Greek paganism. One God — many faiths: monotheism, such as Judaism, Christianity and Islam. One God — one faith: **theomonism** as a synthesis of world religions.

> Monotheistic religions share a faith in one God that will ultimately lead them to unity, i.e. to **theomonism**. The more various faiths approach the truth of Oneness, the closer they are to each other.

Society and Politics

ambi-utopia *n* (Lat *ambi-*, both, on both sides + *utopia*) – a genre that combines utopia and anti-utopia, i.e. ambivalent about certain social ideals and their potential realization.

Ambi-utopianism is a controversial vision of the future. Thomas More was a utopianist, George Orwell, an anti-utopianist; on the other hand, the work of Andrei Platonov (1899–1951) is hard to define in these opposite terms as it combines dreams of the bright communist future with horrifying images of human degradation and atrocity. His novels *Chevengur* and *The Foundation Pit* are good examples of **ambi-utopia**.

> I love technology for the cheap comfort it provides, and I hate it for the very same reason. My next novel about technomania will be definitely an **ambi-utopia**.

ambi-utopian *adj* — related to **ambi-utopia** or **ambi-utopianism**.

> **ambi-utopian** attitude, manifesto, platform, novel, treatise...

crazy cracy, or **crazy-cracy** *n* (*crazy* + *cracy*, from Gr *kratos*, power) — a scornful name for a political regime.

> There is no cause good enough to kill people. Democracy, autocracy, aristocracy... All these **crazy-cracies** are not

worth a single human life.

Matthew has decided to launch a new political movement. He believes that another **crazy-cracy** will make a difference.

deadvertise *v* (*dead* + *advertise*) — to advertise and promote political causes by death.

Terrorism is the art of **deadvertising**.

dreadvertise *v* (*dread* + *advertise*) — to advertise by dread, to engage in propaganda by speading fears and mistrust.

There are skilled **dreadvertisers** in our government.

globotomy *n* (*globe* + *lobotomy*) — aggressive "surgical" solutions to global problems.

The war in Iraq may tear the world apart and lead to **globotomy**.

the dooming 2000s — a nickname for our decade.

The booming 1990s, **the dooming 2000s**.

Americans divide their cultural history into decades: the prosperous fifties, the rebellious sixties, the egoistic seventies, the greedy eighties, the booming nineties. We live in **the dooming 2000s**.

the oopsies, or **the OOpsies** (from *oops*) — a nickname for the 2000s.

The *oops* of surprise and dismay is suggested by the ending zeroes of the decade of big failures and grave mistakes. We failed to detect and avert the terrorist plot — oops. We failed to capture Osama — oops. Iraqi WMD — oops. We promised better life to Iraqis — oops. Our thriving market economy turned out to be a bubble — oops. Thus, **2000-psies**, or **OOpsies**, or **oopsies**.

obamanna *n* (*Obama* + *manna*, from the Bible) — high expectations of miracles that Barack Obama may produce as the U.S. president.

Don't expect **obamanna** immediately falling upon us after the inauguration.

politicosis (cf. *toxicosis*, *psychosis*, etc.) – obsession with politics, propensity to talk politics or politicize everything without adequate knowledge or understanding.

As a young man, John suffered from **politicosis**, but now he hardly even looks into newspapers.

taxicosis *n* (*taxes* + *toxicosis*) — a seasonal depression caused by tax preparation that affects the majority of US population every March and early April. Symptoms: fatigue, nausea, melancholy, etc.

You look depressed. What happened? — A usual spring **taxicosis**.

totalgia *n* (*total* + Gr *nostalgia*) — nostalgic aspiration for totality, national unity, the ideals of social commonality aligned with traditional values and beliefs.

In postcommunist countries, many experience **totalgia**, longing for the lost ideal of social integrity.

Totalitarianism in Russia is still alive in the **totalgia** for the old Soviet customs, songs and morale.

Time

chronocide *n* (Gr *khronos*, time + Lat *cidum*, from *caedere*, to slay; cf. *genocide*, *homicide*) — "the murder of time," the violent disruption of historical continuity.

> Any revolution is a form of **chronocide**: it sacrifices the past and present to the future.

> Communism and fascism are both **chronocidal**: one destroys traditions as it leaps to the chimerical future, another brings the society under the spell of the mythic past.

chronocracy *n* (Gr *chronos*, time + Gr *kratia*, power or rule) — social and political order based on timing; rule by the laws and force of temporality; a form of government imposing time constraints on all authorities and the necessity for periodic transfer of powers on all levels.

Under **chronocracy**, life is determined by the regular periodic change of political, economic, and cultural trends, methods, fashions, and personnel. Presidents, computers, car models, artistic styles, dress cuts, textbooks have to change periodically to maintain their status as "new."

> Who rules in America, *demos* or *chronos*? America is a **chronocracy** no less than a democracy, with strictly enforced changes on all levels, from political leaders to dress fashions and technology.

chronomania *n* (Gr *chronos*, time + Gr *mania*, obsession, madness) — obsession with time and speed; inclination to utilize every moment and to submit one's life to a total time control.

> America suffers from **chronomania**. Faster, faster, faster! Let's pause to see where we stand and consider where exactly we have been rushing headlong.

> **Chronomania** may jeopardize your mental health. Try to refocus your life beyond schedules and deadlines.

chronomaniac *n* — a person obsessed with time and speed who tries to live faster and micro-manage time. Synonym: **timenik** *n* (*time* + suffix *–nik*)

> He checks his watch every minute, a real **chronomaniac**.

> My colleagues are crazy **timeniks**. No one has a minute for a human conversation.

chronopathy *n* (Gr *khronos*, time + Gr *patheia*, suffering) — a temporality disorder, a lack of time sense; inability to manage time, to meet schedules and deadlines.

> **Chronopathy** is the undiagnosed cause of many social disorders and career failures.

> **Chronopathy** can be compared to blindness or dyslexia. An impairment of the time orientation ability, it should be treated as a psychological condition rather than a moral deficiency.

chronopath *n* — a person affected by chronopathy.

> You are always late. Are you a **chronopath**?

chronopathic *adj* — related to **chronopathy**.

> He misses one appointment after another not because of ill intentions or disrespect. He has been **chronopathic** since childhood.

chronosome *n* (Gr *chronos*, time + Gr *soma*, body; cf. *chromosome*) — a unit of historical heredity.

Chromosomes pass the genetic code to subsequent generations; **chronosomes** pass a mental code of a historical period through styles, traditions, and "cultural color."

> The **chronosomes** of the early 20th century avant-garde reached the generation of the 1960s and shaped its political views and artistic styles.

> Young people in the 2000s have different **chronosomes** than we had in the 1990s.

> The **chronosomic** analysis of Finnegans Wake lays bare multiple mythological sources and images of ancient chronicles in Joyce's enigmatic prose.

ex *v trans* (from the Greek derived prefix *ex*, out, from, out of, as in *ex-president*, *ex-husband*) — to make outdated, obsolete, to relegate to the past.

He **exed** his girlfriend and now feels lonely.

Those prone to **exing** others should be ready to be **exed** themselves.

liveline *n* (cf. *deadline*) — the start date of a process. **Liveline** and deadline are the scheduled beginning and the end of an action or procedure.

> The deadline for filing applications is March 31. The **liveline** for application processing is April 1.

> What is the **liveline** for ordering this still unpublishhed book on Amazon?

to ride the edge — to be ahead in something, to be on a cutting edge and take the risks of being first and leading others.

> A recent graduate in quantum physics, Amalia now **rides the edge** of nanotechnology.

timenik *n* (*time* + suffix *–nik*) — see **chronomaniac**.

uchronia *n* (Gr *ou*, not + Gr *chronos*, time; literally "no time"; cf. *utopia*, no place) — a condition of "no time," an uneventful state of permanence.

> As soon as utopia finds its way into reality, it turns into **uchronia**, a disruption of history itself.

> The worlds of great visionaries are often **uchronian**. Perfection precludes change.

Internet and Information Technology

corputer (Lat *corpus*, body + *computer*) — a digital device implanted into the human body; a futuristic term referring to an organ of the cyborg.

> **Corputers** will soon exceed traditional computers in computational power.

EGG *n* (abbreviation) — *Electronically Generated Group*, such as a *smart mob* (*flashmob*) or *bookcrossing* enthusiasts. These communities emerge in cyberspace and use the web to establish social bonds, to connect and act together in real time and space.

> Rapidly emerging **EGGs** take advantage of the speed and flexibility of the web to extend virtual communities into the real world. These **EGGs** are indeed the eggs of new web-initiated communities.

egger *n* — a member of EGG.

> Do you participate in any **EGG**? — Yes, I am a seasoned **egger**.

egonetics *n* (*ego* + *net* + suffix -*ics*) — searching one's own name and creating a network of self-references to increase one's presence on the Web.

Egonetics is a purposeful dissemination of one's name, making links to one's homepage, joining interactive sites, blogs, and forums to boost self-representation. Unless intended for intellectual participation or professional advancement, this is a narcissistic pursuit.

> It is hard to tell where the professional ambitions turn **egonetic**. He just loves seeing himself on the Web and spends hours every day on **egonetics**.

egonetic *n* — a person who engages in **egonetics**.

> Jim is a caring guy and not an egoist in the traditional sense, he is simply an **egonetic**. He loves his name more than himself and is more attached to his virtual persona than to physical existence.

> **Egonetic** doesn't necessarily mean egocentric. In the illusory world of the Web one is desperate for a grip of reality which is one's own name. For an **egonetic**, hu's proper name is the umbilical cord connecting the vast infosphere with the small human being who peeks though the screen.

headmade *adj* (cf. *handmade*) — produced by human mind, or "natural" intelligence rather than by intelligent machines, robotic minds, software programs, etc.

> In the future age of artificial intelligence, **headmade** things will be valued as high as handmade objects in the industrial age of mass production.

humy, or **humie** *n* (diminutive from *human*) — a patronizing name for humans; a human being as an inferior partner of robots or other creatures of superior intelligence. The term also alliterates with "humiliated," the role humans might assume in a technosociety dominated by artificial intelligence.

> For somebody as smart as this **humy**, you have to wonder why he cannot conquer illness and death.

> An average artificial physicist of the 22nd century may look condescendingly even at the brightest **humies** of the past, like Newton and Einstein.

infopause *n* (*information* + *pause*) — a break in using Internet and other sources of information in order to recover from its influx.

> An **infopause** may take from several minutes to months, depending on the gravity of the affliction.

> Every business should introduce at least two five-minute **infopauses** during the workday, with all computers and lights turned off to refresh employees' ability to process new information.

InteLnet (*intellect* + *internet*) — intellectual network; the electronic network at the service of intellectual communication.

InteLnet is an intellectual replica of the Internet, an attempt to connect electronically connectable cyberspaces on intellectual and spiritual levels, and to bring the humanistic message of the Internet in line with electronic media and inter-connectedness of cyberspace. **InteLnet** is a response of the creative mind to the challenge of the expanding electronic universe.

74

InteLnet was launched in 1995 as an experimental site and virtual community to discuss and promote interdisciplinary ideas in the humanities.

netify *v trans* (*net* + suffix *-ify*) — to make something net-like, to give the quality of a net.
Netify differs from "digitize"; it means introducing the features of electronic networks into social communication, into the off-line world at large.

We are trying to **netify** the cumbersome structure of our team.

netification *n* — the impact of electronic networks on society, culture, etc.

> The future lies in the **netification** of society, i. e. making it as transparent to mind and open for communication as an electronic network.

netscapism *n* (*net* + *escapism*) - an inclination to retreat from unpleasant realities into the electronic network, or virtual world.

> In the past, the wild nature and remote countries provided the favorite refuge for social escape. Now it is the net. **Netscapism** has grown into a serious problem, especially among adolescents.

netscapist *n* - a person who escapes from unpleasant realities into the networld.

> **Netscapists** are ubiquitous today. If you are texting your roommate instead of talking with him in a living room, you are in danger of becoming a **netscapist**.

socionetics *n* (*social* + *net* + suffix *-ics*) — a discipline that explores socially transformative effects and potentials of electronic networks.

> **Socionetics** studies web communities and the grassroot democracy they generate, as opposed to the bureaucratic style of representative democracy.

technopoeia (Gr *techne*, art, craft + Gr *poiein*, to make or create) — the poetic, visionary side of technology as a form of creativity, as a transformation of the world by laws of harmony and beauty.

> Bridges spanning rivers like man-made rainbows; skyscrapers gleaming in a blue haze; virtual worlds bringing the freedom of fantasy and transformation – all this is **technopoeia**. Technology is every bit as metaphoric and symbolic as poetry, it just expresses its energy not verbally but in form of poetically transformed matter where each element plays with nature, defying gravity and physical constraints.

> Using scientific instruments and communication facilities, **technopoeia** lets us see the invisible, hear the inaudible, speak in tongues, bring our word to every corner of the uni verse, and burst open the vast horizons of land and skies. **Technopoeia** expands the scope of poetry though engineering.

videocracy *n* (Lat *video*, I see + Gr *kratos*, power, rule; cf. *ideocracy*) — the power of visual images in shaping the society; the impact of television, cinema, Internet, and advertising on public opinion, politics, market strategies, etc.

Ideocracy is dead since the ex-communist countries are no longer communist. Was it the power of democratic ideals or American-style videocracy that overwhelmed the communist utopia? **Videocracy** has become indeed an integral part of American democracy in the media age.

videology *n* (Lat *video*, I see + Gr. *logos*, word, thought, doctrine; cf. *ideology*) — the impact of visual media on public mentality, the combined effects of visual information and propaganda.

> The power of ideology that culminated in totalitarian regimes of the 20th century has been successfully contested by the Western art of **videology**: visual images appear to be more convincing than abstract ideas expressed verbally.

vir *n* (*virtual* + Russian *mir*, world) — a virtual world providing full-range sensorial experience so the subject is unable to tell reality from illusion.

> English scientists have recently built the prototype **vir**, a kitchen-size space to experience real virtuality.

> I will not let you go to that **vir** alone: who knows what temptations will you face there.

virtonautics *n* (*virtual* + *nautics*, from Gr *nautikos*, of ships, sailing) — exploration of virtual worlds.

> Our current trips thru the computer screen are just wading along the beach. **Virtonautics** means leaving the shore (=the screen) behind and venturing far into the cyberworld as the emergent 3D environment available to all the five senses.

Virtonautics is still in embryo, but has a potential to become even more common an occupation than aeronautics and astronautics are today.

virtonaut *n* — a person engaged in virtonautics.

Our kids all become **virtonauts** at the earliest age and have hard time switching careers.

webbiage *n* (*web* + suffix *-iage*; cf. *verbiage*) — excessive use of web tools and design beyond what is reasonable to achieve a certain goal.

Why do you need all this **webbiage**? Simplify!

Language

Anglonet *n* (*anglo* + *net*) — the English language sector of the WWW.

> **Anglonet** contains about 227 billion words vs. Runet (Russian network) with just 30 billions.

elonym *n* (*electronic* + Gr *onyma*, name; cf. *pseudonym*) — electronic name; the part of electronic address that precedes @.

> In our corporate mail system, **elonyms** are assigned based on first initial plus the last name with last letter deleted. Mine is bjohnso (Bill Johnson).

> His **elonym** is as pretentious as himself: aaaaa111. Clearly he claims to be alpha, not omega.

Englobal *adj* (*English* + *global*) or **Englobish** (*Engl* + *glob* + *ish*) — the international English, as opposed to national/local variants of the English language, such as British English, American English, Spanglish, etc.

> What language does he speak? It doesn't quite sound English. — It's **Englobal**: not quite English, but still usable almost everywhere in the world.

infinition *n* (*infinity* + *definition*) — an incomplete and potentially infinite definition; the process of defining something that cannot be fully or precisely defined; an open list of possible definitions.

infine *v trans* (Lat *in*, not + *finis*, boundary; cf. *define, refine*) — to define in a negative way something indefinable, to stop or postpone the process of definition.

Certain emergent fluid concepts are subject to **infinition** — infinite dispersal of their meaning — rather than to definition. For example, Lao-tse never says what Tao is but only provides a number of **infinitions**: "The Tao that can be trodden is not the enduring and unchanging Tao. The name that can be named is not the enduring and unchanging name."[6] Jacques Derrida never defines his method of deconstruction but only **infines** it in numerous passages. To **infine** means to suggest multiple possible definitions and state that none of them can define the subject.

There are several ways to **infine** a concept:

1. Directly stating that the concept cannot be fully defined.
2. Providing multiple definitions that succeed and cancel each other thus amounting to a long **infinition**.
3. Providing an inconsistent, paradoxical definition that points out the mutually exclusive properties of the concept (such as "perfection" and "evolution").

---

6. *The Tao Te Ching,* ch. 1, 1-2.

The need for **infinitions** can be inferred from Gödel's theorems. The most basic concepts of any philosophical or religious system, such as God, Being, Absolute, Spirit, Beauty, Love, are not definable within these systems. Each discipline has its own primary concepts subject to **infinitions**, such as *wisdom* in philosophy, *soul* in psychology, or *word* in linguistics.

interlation *n* (*inter* + *lation*; cf. *translation*) — variation of a theme in two or more languages; unlike in translation, the roles of source and target languages are interchangeable; a verbal art based on figurative (metaphoric) relationship between languages.

Robert Frost said that poetry is what gets lost in translation. **Interlation** synergistically increases poetic value by adding more layers of imagery to metaphors of each language.

> Bilingual people don't need translation but may enjoy an **interlation**, e.g., two juxtaposed language versions of apparently identical texts – say, a Joseph Brodsky's poem in Russian and English. His own translation of his Russian line meaning "Loneliness is a man squared" into English reads: "Loneliness cubes a man at random." It would be irrelevant to ask which of these expressions is more adequate to Brodsky's thought. This Russian-English **interlation** represents the scope of its metaphoric meaning.

Silentese *n* or *adj* (*silent* + suffix *–ese*, as in Chinese, Portuguese) — the language of silence; may use non-verbal signs, gestures, mimicry, or facial expressions.

> He didn't say anything. — Why, he spoke eloquently, but in **Silentese**, the most difficult language to study and

understand.

We are working on a **Silentese**-English dictionary. It translates into English the hidden messages of our mind and the meanings of our silence and pauses for which so far we have no vocabulary.

stereotext *n* (Gr *stereo*, three-dimensional + *text*; cf. *stereo music*, *stereo cinema*) — multilingual writing using multiple languages to convey the multidimensionality of thought and imagery by emphasizing the variety of associative connections.

The stereo effect may be either intentional or achieved by the experience of reading multiple versions of the same text. Vladimir Nabokov's autobiography can be read as a **stereo-text** in two languages and three consecutive versions: *Conclusive Evidence* (1951) — *Drugie berega* (1954) — *Speak, Memory* (1964). Nabokov pointed out that these are much more than mere translations: "This re-Englishing of a Russian re-vision of what had been an English re-telling of Russian memories in the first place, proved to be a diabolical task, but some consolation was given me by the thought that such multiple metamorphosis, familiar to butterflies, had not been tried by any human before."[4]

In a global society, "**stereo textuality**" can be viewed not just as an odd by-product of the growing multilingualism, but as the most adequate form of verbal creativity. Stereo music and stereo cinema (3D films) reproduce sounds and images better than the "mono" technology. **Stereotext** has the same quality: properly presenting an idea and conveying all the dimensions of thought and imagery may take at least two languages, like two eyes or two ears. The synergy of languages yields **stereo poetry** or **stereo prose**.

textoid *n* (*text* + Gr suffix *-oid* referring to likeness; cf. *asteroid*) — a virtual, digital text that can be edited by any user and exists only while being read.

The digital era shattered the traditional concept of text. Once immutable, self-identical texts are turning into fluid, dynamic, transient **textoids** roaming the web and constantly modified by users, much like an epic song in a traditional community.

> Wikipedia is a collection of permanently revised **textoids** that never settle as stable texts.

tonguefusion *n* (cf. *transfusion*) — a fusion of languages, in a literary work or otherwise.

> Joyce's *Finnegans Wake* is a perfect example of **tonguefusion**.

verbject *n* (*verbal* + *object*) — a verbal object: (1) a smart computerized object that is managed by verbal commands; (2) a genre of art that combines a material object and a text into one whole.

> Yesterday things were silent, today **verbjects** listen and respond. Even a freezer has its own raspy voice.

> In Conceptualist **verbjects**, the physical presence of the objects, such as a chair or a spade, complements the text that describes them in documentary or imaginative ways.

Grammatical Words
(conjunction, pronoun)

bespite *conj* (*because* + *despite*) — "because of or in spite of" in condensed form.

> This book will generate keen interest in both scholars and the general public, **bespite** its controversial nature.

> **Bespite** the intensity of the debate, there has been major progress in our understanding of this trend.

> **Bespite** the expectation of Truman's imminent defeat, Democrats turned out in numbers and assured his victory.

hu *pron* (from *human*) — a gender-neutral third person pronoun.

Hu is a back-clipping (a word's shortened form with the end omitted, like *lab*, *math*, *ad*, or *condo*).

Hu is pronounced (hju:), like in *human*, and is thus close to two other person-related genderless singular pronouns, *you* and *who*. *Who* and **hu** are naturally drawn to each other by rhyming and communicational contexts, as a question and the answer. **Hu** points to that generic, genderless **hu**man to whom the Who? refers. The answer is prompted by the question itself. "Who buys this stuff? Who would want a car like that?" — "Anyone who believes that **hu** can afford it."

The forms of the third person pronouns are:

	Nom	Gen/Adj	Acc	Refl
Masculine	he	his	him	himself
Feminine	she	her	her	herself
Neutral	hu	hu's	hu	huself

Anyone stating that **hu** has a conflict of interests should not serve as an investigator.

An employee may choose to cover only **huself** and **hu's** child or any number of children.

It's the vice-president's job to support the president and take **hu's** place when **hu** is away.

A university professor must exhibit **huself** in **hu's** own true character — that is, as an ignorant human being, actively utilizing **hu's** small share of knowledge.

An introvert can easily become an extrovert when it is advantageous for **hu** to do so.

To avoid gender bias, some prefer switching to plural. However, such a solution is problematic and may compromise the language's ability to deal with individuals. Compare:

A hero is one who places **huself** at risk for another.
vs.
Heroes are those who place themselves at risk for others.

To convey this idea I would like to imagine **a** hero, one human being rather than a group, a mass of heroes. Resorting to they eliminates not only gender, but individuality as well. Should we speak and think about people as multitudes only? It is important to talk about a student, an employee, an author, a doctor, a physicist, or a person, rather than to refer to faceless students, authors, doctors, persons, etc. Better to adjust the grammar to ethical and conceptual concerns, not the other way around. Gaining gender-neutral grammar at the expense of an individual reference is a dubious achievement.

Hu has several advantages over other applicants for the job:

1. **Hu** is fully motivated and semantically/ etymologically justified as a short form of *human*. Whenever **hu** is used, human resonates behind it making it memorable, meaningful and suggestive (unlike artificial pronouns suggested earlier, such as *e, et, mon, na, ne, po, se, tey*).

2. **Hu** is a two-letter one-syllable word. Using **hu** instead of "he or she" (2 keystrokes *vs.* 9), **huself** instead of "himself or herself," etc. saves time, space, and effort, especially in e-mail.

3. **Hu** follows the pattern of the pronouns *he* and *she* (same 'h,' a single vowel, open syllable) and is thus their good partner in gender specialization within a lexical family.

4. **Hu** is spelled consistently with pronunciation, unlike the unpronounceable *s/he*.

5. **Hu**, unlike *they* used to refer to an individual, is not grammatically disruptive and can be used routinely and mechanically, without twisting the sentence to put everything in plural.

6. **Hu** easily lends itself to derivatives following the common patterns, e.g., **hu's** and **huself**.
7. To borrow a gender-neutral pronoun from another language, we may consider the Old English *ou*, Persian *u*, and Arabic *hu* already used in this role. Any of them could be easily incorporated into contemporary English, adding (or keeping) the *h*, as a short form of the genderless *human*.

So far, I see no strong arguments against **hu**-language, the language of undivided **hu**manness. In the near future, this humanness will require to be even better articulated to distinguish our species from any artificial forms of intelligence emerging to assume ever more active roles in civilization and language. Soon we'll have to answer questions like "Who is doing this or that (reading, speaking, thinking, etc.)?" The answer may be either **hu** (human) or *it* (machine). We need the word *hu* not only to harmonize the verbal treatment of men and women, but also to tell apart human vs. non-human beings that will increasingly share qualities, environments, and jobs. We need that word to refer to a human agent in the context of human/machine interaction.

In a famous episode of *Star Trek: The Next Generation*, the Enterprise's crew liberate an individual from the evil Borg Collective and give **hu**, of course, the name Hu(gh). **Hu**(gh) is indeed so human.

“   ”

Medium and Margin: The Reversal

I offer a new sign that signifies the absence of any sign and is conveyed by the pair of quotation marks around the blank space.

I speak about the blank space that surrounds and underlies the text and about the way we can present it within the text and make it the focus of our thinking.

Any text has its medium and margin. What if their roles, prescribed by these names, were reversed and the margin found itself within the medium? (By "margins," in the broad sense, I mean also the background of the text).

The margin placed within the medium looks like "   ", if we choose to designate the boundaries of this blank space with quotation marks.

"   " is a citation

The role of quotation marks is to recognize the usage (incorporation, repetition) of a source external to the given text.

However, the text of this section cites not some other text, but its own margin, the environment that makes this text possible, visible, writable, and readable.

By putting the blank space in quotation marks we reverse the relationship between the "inside" and "outside" of the text. The outside moves into the inside.

My way of introducing "   " in an oral presentation is a short interval of silence marked by air quotes.

Medium and Margin

This simple scheme shows how the margins move inside the
medium and are delimited within it by quotation marks.

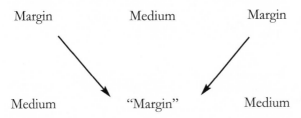

Text and Environment

In the same way, the environment of the text moves inside the
text and becomes one of its elements, a textual sign demarcated
by quotation marks.

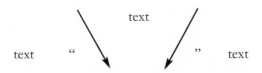

The Environment of the Text

The paper on which the text is written or printed, or the canvas of a painting, or the screen of a computer, forms the environment of the text.

The margins and the background of the text constitute not only its environment but also the precondition of its possibility to be written and read.

The text of this section is self-reflective. It incorporates its own margin and stages a visual and semiotic experiment with one non-verbal sign: "   ".

This sign transforms the environment of the text into one of its components, a new sign that functions among other textual signs.

Indexical Sign

The sign "   " is not a symbolic or an iconic
sign, like letters or pictures. It belongs to the third, indexical
variety of signs (Ch. Pierce's triadic classification).

An index is a part (a cause or an effect) of what it signifies, like
smoke is an index of a fire or dark clouds are an index of
impending rain. Indexes are ubiquitous in nature but almost
never appear on printed pages, for example, in books or albums.

"   " is the only textual indexical sign I can think
of, because it signifies that empty background which underlies
each text and makes it visible and articulate. "   "
is itself a part of what it signifies, it belongs to this pure, white
"ether" that surrounds the text, like dark clouds belong to the
rainy weather.

Through this transparent   "   " we see directly
the background, but within the quotation marks it becomes a
sign of itself.

The Beyond of the Text:
Relativity and Universality

Ludwig Wittgenstein: "What can be shown, cannot be said"
(Tractatus).

In "   ", language shows its beyond, that tran-
scendent region of the world which cannot be said in language,
but can only be shown. We can see "   ", but we
cannot say it. While ceasing to speak, language begins to show,
operating as an index and pointing to the environment beyond
itself.

What appears within the quotes varies from one medium to
another (it may be white or blue, paper or screen, sand or
stone), but in each case "   " represents the con-
dition specific to its particular medium. On the white it is white,
on the blue it is blue.

It is co-substantial with its medium, which makes this sign both
relative and universal.

"   " is the same everywhere, in each language,
on each surface, precisely because it points to the given surface;
it directly manifests "the beyond" of the text through its inter-
nal gap.

Search for the Ultimate Sign

From antiquity, philosophical and linguistic thought has been looking for a sign that could adequately convey that which conditions the very existence or possibility of signs.

There are many words to designate the ultimate nature of everything: "Being", "Absolute", "Idea", "Oneness", "Essence", "Nothing", "Infinity", "Unnamable", "Tao", "Différance"…

For example, according to Heidegger, in order to name this "beingness of being," language has to find something unique, "this singular word." For Heidegger, such a unique word is Greek "   ," "being."

However, even the most universal verbal signs that express the infinite and inexhaustible nature of being are not adequate to their intended signifieds, because these signs are symbolic, conditional and arbitrary.

Lao Tse: "Tao that can be expressed in words is not a permanent Tao."

Derrida: "'Older' than being itself, such a différance has no name in our language. … If it is unnamable, it is not provisionally so, not because our language has not yet found or received this name, or because we would have to seek it in another language… It is rather because there is no name for it at all, not even the name of essence or of being, not even that of 'dif-férance' …"

Indeed, "   " or "différance"– each of these words is only one among many, a combination of Greek or Latin characters. None of them has any privilege over other names in other languages in designating the very condition of naming.

"   " in Philosophy

The philosophical language game can go on forever searching for a single name that transcends the contingency and arbitrariness of verbal signs. A primordial and universal principle cannot be expressed with verbal signs, but it cannot remain unexpressed either. Philosophy is the most general investigation into the nature of the world and a search for fundamental concepts to express it.

A fundamental concept can be articulated only at the frontier of language. It cannot be within language, given the arbitrariness of language; it cannot be outside language, because then it would not be a sign. At the frontier of language may be a sign both inside and outside that can express the nonspeakable condition of speakability, the nonverbal condition of verbality.

"   " is adequate for this purpose because, as both sign and index, it manifests the conditions of both signification and indication.

"   " speaks the most universal language, that of the blank space.

"   " gives a name to what creates a condition for naming.

"   " is a more adequate and universal term for the Absolute or the Infinite than the words absolute and infinite, which are composed of certain letters in a certain language.

Negative Semiotics
and Apophatic Theology

I call "   " a (non)sign because it emerges on
the boundary of text and non-text. It is an indexical sign, but
from the point of view of symbolic signs that constitute the
language, it is not a sign.

The (non)sign "   " belongs to the field of neg-
ative semiotics and corresponds to the concept of unknowable,
invisible, indefinable God in apophatic theology. Contrary to
cataphatic theology that aims to present God in positive terms,
like "light," "strength," "reason", "perfection," apophatic theolo-
gy ascends to God and speaks about God through silence and
darkness, through non-visibility and non-speakability.

In apophatic terms, this Final Cause, as Pseudo-Dionysius
Areopagite called God, can be designated as "
" of theology.

The oral equivalent of "   " is a pause as an
articulate unit of silence.

One can apply "   " as a universal semiotic con-
cept in any subject area, not only philosophy or theology. Each
discipline has its own "unspeakable" conditions and assump-
tions that need to be presented within the discipline. At the
same time such conditions and assumptions need to be hidden

from presentation because they remain transcendent to what they make possible. That is why we need negative semiotics, the semiotics of (non)signs.

Ecology of Text

There is a parallel in the relationships between text and non-text and between culture and nature.

The nature is usually posited as the outside of culture, as its preexisting condition and environment.

Ecology, as an ethical concern and social activity, attempts to turn the "outside" of culture into its "inside." "National parks," "wild refuges," "natural sanctuaries" become the zones of nature inside civilization, protected by civilization from civilization itself.

This shift is paralleled in ecologically conscious philology, linguistics, and literary and cultural studies by the same transformation of the text's environment into its interior area, " ". Here quotation marks function similarly to the boundaries of natural sanctuaries within industrial settings and developmental areas.

"   " is an island of environmental purity, a sanctuary of "non-text" within the text.

Ecophilology (1)

Ecophilology is a discipline that explores the role of textual environments in various settings, in all kinds of media, from the ancient cave drawings and graffiti to the contemporary electronic media.

What follows is a list of some issues and problems of ecophilology:

The number of printed signs per square meter of living space as a measure of semiotic saturation of space. The semiotic load of offices, streets, public places, different cities and countries. Textual capacity of the space -- a number of posters, billboards, slogans, announcements, street signs per square mile or other units of territory.

The length of texts. The size of a text as an ecological factor. With the increase of textual production (informational explosion) the size of the texts that compete for readership has to decrease. The number of classics, the texts that must be read, increases, and accordingly increases the number of "uneducated" people unable to read "all classics."

Ecophilology (2)

Ecology of various genres. Fragment and aphorism are ecologically pure genres: a tiny text among vast virgin blank spaces.

Chronotope and ecology. The term "the space of the novel" has a double meaning: its internal ("described") and external ("occupied") space. Intratextual chronotopes -- a system of spatial and temporal imagery: how it is related to the extratextual chronotopes, the spatial and temporal extension of the text itself. The volume of the book, the multiplication of volumes of the same work. Ecology of book series, of anthologies, encyclopedias, complete works. Each of these megatextual wholes has its own environmental dimension.

Non-reading as a passive resistance to semiocracy (the power of signs). Out of ten messages coming by e-mail, seven or eight end up in the trashcan, but to determine which ones we need a certain amount of time. This is an important factor -- time needed for the detection of textual waste; reading necessary for establishing that reading is unnecessary. Increase of semiotic procedures required for non-participation in semiotic processes. How much do we need to read in order not to read? Minus-time and minus-space of culture.

Verse and Prose

The difference between poetry and prose derives from their various interaction with "   ". The variable, broken, zigzag-like layout of lines is characteristic of poetry, where the relationship between the text and "   " changes from line to line.

> All happy families
> resemble one another;
> every unhappy family
> is unhappy in its own way.

In verses "   " is much more expansive, occupying the larger part of the page, and it is more active: each line has its own zone of the "unsaid" and "undersaid." This zone is resilient, now contracting and now expanding in the inverse relationship with the length of lines.

Although the text above is actually the beginning of Leo Tolstoy's novel *Anna Karenina*, due to this layout it reads as poetry because the structure of its intentionality becomes different. The variation of blank spaces on the sides of the lines increases the intensity of the semantic expectation. The potentiality of meaning exceeds the actual meaning.

"   "

and Eco-Ethics

The ethical relationship has two main aspects: as a relationship to the parental, to what precedes and creates us; and as a relationship to the neighborly, to what co-exists and interacts with us. Hence, the two greatest commandments: "love thy Lord" and "love your neighbor." In this respect, nature presents a double ethical object: in relation to humans, it is both mother (progenitor) and neighbor (environment).

Through "   " a text fulfills its ethical relationship with what both precedes and surrounds it, by acknowledging and incorporating them.

The ethics of the relationship between the text and "
" may serve as a model for other aspects of human activities. We not only write and read, but also speak, eat, drink, breathe, love, and live. Each of these activities has its own "
", the precondition that makes our actions possible.

The precondition of eating is hunger, i.e., the need in "daily bread." To honor this precondition, people fast. Fasting is not a hunger in its primordial state; it is a sign of hunger, a citation of hunger within the "gastronomic" text of our life. Fasting is the "   " of eating.

" "
Yoga and Meditation

Another precondition of our life is the instinct of breathing. It is honored in yoga by holding one's breath, thus making the precondition of breathing a self-referential sign in the "respirational" text of our life.

Yoga also develops those kinds of meditation that reveal the " " of our consciousness by restoration within it its own precondition: non-consciousness. A yogi is not unconscious in the sense in which stones or plants are unconscious. He is consciously unconscious as he reproduces, or quotes the "unconscious" in the text of his consciousness.

Meditation can be viewed as the search for " " in the text(ure) of our life, as a reverential practice of citing the preconditions of our existence.

" " is a sort of textual yoga, a meditation on textuality which attempts to restore and honor its precondition. This text, with many "clean zones" on it surface, is an experiment in textual fasting and self-purification through the sign of " ".

Exposure and Concealment

"　　　　　　　" allows us to speak ethically about any primary condition, without objectifying and verbalizing it in terms of its own consequences. The white that makes text visible is reciprocally made visible through "　　　　　　　". It is both exposed and concealed, in the double gesture of gratitude and reverence.

"　　　　　　　" should not be verbalized (lexicalized, phoneticized), i.e., forcefully appropriated by the text. Ethics presumes incorporation without appropriation.

Alan Badiou: "Evil in this case is to want, at all costs and under condition　　of a truth, to force the naming of the unnameable. Such, exactly, is the principle of disaster." (Ethics. An Essay on the Understanding of Evil)

"White Paintings" of
Robert Rauschenberg

In Visual Art

" " played an important role in many art movements of the 20th century. It was presented as an unpainted canvas, pure background left unfinished in the completed work. The background moves forward and takes the place of the foreground.

A radical experiment of representation of the original blank canvas is found in the "White Paintings" of Robert Rauschenberg exhibited at the Black Mountain College in 1953. The painting exposes its own preconditions, something that it usually hides under the layers of paint.

The next stage in the evolution of this "void-art" is its progression from an individual work to the entire exhibition space. A landmark of artistic environmentalism can be seen in Yves Klein's notorious exhibition "The Void" (Paris, 1958), which consisted of empty, whitewashed walls.

Kazimir Malevich
"White on White"
(1918)

"   "

in Malevich

Kazimir Malevich, the father of Suprematism, can be also considered the founder of margin-into—medium art (the art that transforms visual margin into medium). His painting "White on White" (1918) is an image of the background only slightly contrasted with the background itself, which in its turn may be an image of a larger background that surrounds the painting (a wall in the exhibition hall or a computer monitor in a Power Point presentation).

This case of a double visual citation, a citation of a citation, can be compared with the smaller "   " placed within larger
"   ".

"   "   "   "   "

It is possible to present "   " in different sizes, one within another, like Russian dolls. The citational mode (both visual and textual) can be continued and multiplied ad infinitum.

As there is intentional blankness within blankness, there is also silence within silence, which can be revealed and cited in a deep conversation.

Ilya Kabakov.
"At the Big Artistic Council"
(1983)

           "   **"**

in Conceptualism

Conceptualism departs from the traditional art by introducing into visual space, on the one hand, texts, and, on the other hand, emptiness. Conceptualism crosses the borders of visual representation simultaneously in these two "non-visual" directions: extra-language ("   ") and alter-language (words). Even in a work of visual art, text and "   " appear to gravitate to each other in their opposition to visuality itself. Extra-language and alter-language are correlated and balanced, words pointing to what remains empty and unseen.

In Ilya Kabakov's work "At the Big Artistic Council" (1983), the area of words presupposes and defies the area of emptiness. The reader-viewer learns about the painting of a football game and the discussion at the artistic council only from the detailed caption, while in place of the image we find the smooth white surface (with only one almost imperceptible image of a ball). The verbal description corresponds to the blank canvas.

John Cage
4'33"
(1952)

in Music

A musical manifestation (and a manifesto) of   "
" is found in the composition 4'33"by the American avant-garde
composer John Cage. The score instructs the performer not to
play any instrument in the duration of the piece. Although com-
monly perceived as "four minutes thirty-three seconds of
silence," the composition actually consists of the sounds of the
environment that the listeners hear while it is (non) performed.
Thus, again, the outside of the text moves to its inside, to
become framed as a separate musical piece.

"   " in Literature.
V. Gnedov, "The Long Poem of the End"
(1913)

One of the earliest examples of "   " in a literary work is "Poema kontsa" ("The Long Poem of the End") by Russian avant-garde poet Vasilisk Gnedov (1890 – 1978). This poem concludes his collection "Smert' iskusstvu" ("Death to Art," 1913) and consists of one page that, except for the title, number, and the publisher's seal at the bottom, is left blank.

While performing it, "Gnedov would raise his arm and then quickly let it fall in a dramatic gesture, eliciting stormy applause from the audience" (Adrian Wanner). Another witness, Ivan Ignatiev, cites a rhythmic gesticulation of Gnedov's hand from left to right and vice versa, in such a way that one movement nullified the other and symbolically presented a void, a self-erasure.

Please, look below at the clean page as presented in
Gnedov's poem. It is a poem, and it needs to be read.
Let us look attentively into it and read it.
Don't you feel a kind of dizziness?

The Paradox of Invisibility

If we look at certain objects, such as a white wall or a blue tablecloth, we see colors that are part of physical space. However, we cannot contemplate in the same way, as a material surface, the blank white paper or the blank blue screen that serve as a background for signs, as a semiotic vacuum, zero level of semioticity. We do not look at them, we look into them, and, the more we look, the more we lose the object of contemplation. Whiteness and blueness are no longer colors of the material surface, but the depth of the sign-continuum that is essentially colorless as pure potentiality of signs and meaning.

We experience a kind of dizziness when we stop simply looking at the blank paper (which is perfectly visible) and strive to read its blankness. We try to fathom the semiotic vacuum that invites reading and simultaneously denies it by the absence of signs. This loss of orientation in the semiotic vacuum is the cause of dizziness.

The Metaphysics of
" "

in Melville

H. Melville, Moby Dick: "But not yet have we solved the incantation of this whiteness and learned why it appeals with such power to the soul. ...Is it that by its indefiniteness it shadows forth the heartless voids and immensities of the universe, and thus stabs us from behind with the thought of annihilation, when beholding the white depths of the Milky Way? Or is it, that as in essence whiteness is not so much a color as the visible absence of color, and at the same time the concrete of all colors; is it for these reasons that there is such a dumb blankness, full of meaning, in a wide landscape of snows...?"

(ch.42. "The Whiteness of The Whale")

Phenomenology of

"   "

From a blank paper or screen our vision gets a mixed signal: to look at the text, not at the material surface; but it is only the surface that we find there, not the text. Thus we feel blinded by our overstrained look beyond the colored surface, into the semiotic void, i.e., into the absent, purely intentional object of reading.

What we are reading in this blankness is the intentionality of discourse as such, its phenomenological writability and readability, though it remains factually unwritten and unread, without any text on it.

From the phenomenological point of view, the blankness of a paper or a screen is a mode of notation not of specific letters, but of the very intention of writing or reading. We deal here with purely intentional semiotic objects. This intentionality deepens our perception of a blank page or screen so that we begin to see in it the very invisibility of what we are looking into, and simultaneously don't see the seeable, the surface.

Semiotic Vacuum
White Holes

If we want to learn how to read in the full meaning of this word, we need to read the potentiality of writing, not only its actualization in letters.

Introduced into a text, "   " blows up its code of signification from within and causes a semiotic shock in the reader.

"   " is perceived not as a piece of gray or glossy white paper, but as semiotic nothingness, a white hole that absorbs and annihilates our reading intention.

These white holes of textuality could be regarded as semantic analogues of the black holes in the physical universe.

According to contemporary physics, the so-called vacuum is not vacuous at all. It holds an enormous amount of energy in the form of virtual particles and is seen by some scientists as a limitless source of free energy. Similarly, semiotic "vacuum" holds an enormous amount of energy in the form of virtual words and meanings.

The Semantic Intensity of White Holes

Let us assume the semantic intensity of text to equal one, for an actual sign corresponds to its actual meaning.

Then the semantic intensity of margins approaches zero in the reader's perception because, in the absence of actual signs, there is no expectation of potential signification.

By contrast, the semantic intensity of "   " approaches infinity, as its potential significance is inscribed in text in the absence of an actual sign.

"   " is a singular event in the life of the text. A singularity means a point where some property becomes infinite. For example, at the center of a black hole the density is infinite.

"   " as a white hole is a singularity because it represents the potentially infinite environment of the text condensed in one non-verbal sign with its semantic density approaching infinity.

Transtextual Reading

Try to observe yourself while reading the text full of while holes. Your glance is instinctively drawn to, and repelled by, those holes, sensing in them both destructive and constructive energy that breaks up the text and hinders the perception of its semantic coherence.

Such is the difficulty of our direct encounter with the intentionality of writing when it reveals itself in the rupture of text.

Gradually, the reader develops what can be called transtextual intentionality, i.e., attention to the boundaries of text, to its margins and internal blanks.

How to Pronounce
"   " ?

"   " presents a particular difficulty because we
don't know how to pronounce it (in distinction from the pro-
nounceable terms, like "Absolute," "Tao," or "Being").

As we attempt to pronounce "   ", we catch our-
selves filling this pause with some non-phonetic sound, like
"mhm" or "eh," which stops abruptly, recognizing its lack of
motivation and a failure of full articulation.

"   " functions in our internal speech as a mecha-
nism of disruption. The intention to pronounce "
" cannot realize itself in any phonetically motivated form. Thus
"   " presents itself as a barrier between
potentiality and actuality of speech formation.

How to Verbalize
" " ?

At first we look for ways to fill "   " in a tradi-
tional lexical and morphological manner, e.g. searching through
synonyms (mostly nouns) and choosing a word that seems more
appropriate in a certain context, such as "blank," "whiteness,"
"void" and "emptiness." We start articulating this word-substi-
tute in place of "   ".

Soon, however, we realize that a substitution appropriate for
one context does not fit in the others. Slowly, through alterna-
tion of various contexts, "   " is purified in our
perception of all fillers and reveals its unique meaning in its
wholeness, its holeness, its semiotic "holiness," as the sign of
pure (un)pronounceability, (un)readability, and (un)writability,
for which there can be no substitute among verbal signs.

"   " works as a mechanism of disrupture and
deautomatization, not only of any specific text, but also of tex-
tuality as such.

As a result of this experience of defamiliarization, our relation-
ship with our own internal speech becomes more conscious.

The Double Unconscious of Language: " "

As a Model of Linguistic Self-Awareness

As a rule, we use language unconsciously, and language itself, according to Jacques Lacan, presents the structure of the unconscious. Then the margins that surround text and usually remain unnoticed, as a background, can be conceptualized as the linguistic unconscious of the second order: the unconscious of the unconscious.

By introducing "   " into text, we not only become aware of this double unconscious, but we acquire a new consciousness of language within language. Through this white hole language exposes to our vision and consciousness whatever was previously buried in its invisible and unconscious depths.

History of

["]   ["]

"   " is historical and belongs to the history of
textuality and to the history of consciousness.

Meyer Shapiro: "We take for granted today as indispensable
means the rectangular form of the sheet of paper and its clearly
defined smooth surface on which one draws and writes. But
such a field corresponds to nothing in nature or mental imagery
where the phantoms of visual memory come up in a vague
unbounded void. The student of prehistoric art knows that a
regular field as an advanced artifact presupposes a long develop-
ment of art. The cave paintings of the Old Stone Age are on
unprepared ground, the rough wall of a cave; the irregularities
of earth and rock show through the image. /.../ The smooth
prepared field is an invention of a later stage of humanity."
("On some problems in the semiotics of visual art").

For centuries texts were inscribed into "   ",
which gradually expanded and became more refined, smooth
and clear. This prepared the historical turning point, at which
we can now inscribe "   " into the text.

What is Avant-Garde?

Lyn Hejinian: "A question has arisen among some graduate students at Berkeley as to why there is nothing in academic arts/humanities scholarship that might be comparable to the "avant-garde" in the arts proper. That is the question we hope to explore—what might experimental criticism or avant-garde scholarship look like?" (in an invitation to the conference "Medium and Margin," Berkeley, March 2009).

What is avant-garde? Can this term be applied not only to art and literature, but to theory as well?

The majority of avant-garde movements, including Futurism, Suprematism and Surrealism, emerged from avant-garde theories (manifestos, projects, utopian visions). In many cases, avant-garde theory precedes and shapes avant-garde art.

Avant-garde is a radical experiment with sign systems undermining their foundations and reversing the order of subordination between their centers and peripheries. The crude vs. the gentle, the social vs. the private, technology vs. nature, action vs. contemplation, the abstract vs. the figurative...

Avant-Garde:
The Reversal of Medium and Margin

The reversal of medium and margin is the textual analogue and prototype of all avant-garde reversals.

All aforementioned margin-into-medium authors (from Malevich and Gnedov to Cage to Rauschenberg to Kabakov) belonged to various avant–garde movements, from Futurism to Suprematism to Neo-Dada to Minimalism to Conceptualism. Avant-garde challenges the artistic mainstream and represents a pushing of the boundaries of what is accepted as the norm in art.

The reversal of medium and margin is a signature device of avant-garde.

"   " graphically represents what avant-garde aims for: marginalizing the center and centralizing the periphery, voicing the mute, and uncovering and advancing the suppressed layers of culture.

Avant-Garde in Theory

So far as the humanities deal with texts and textuality, the avant-garde trend in theory would be:

(1) analysis of "   ", which is specific for each discipline, and the explosive role of white holes in various subject areas.

(2) synthesis of new concepts and discovery of new ways of "reversive" and "transformative" thinking and writing.

What happens with the margin and medium if they are reversed and mutually transformed? How texts, sign systems and entire cultures change by incorporating their own outside? What are ethical and aesthetical consequences of this ecological (in the broadest sense) shift? This is a major interest and concern of an avant-garde thinker.

The End (?)

A New Linguistic Turn:
From Analysis to Synthesis

The live vibrant speech we hear ignites our imagination with the fire of new creations, i.e., new word formations... The only duty our vitality imposes on us is creating words... The first experience elicited by the word is conjuring up... phenomena that have never existed; the word gives birth to action... Creating language is the purpose of poetry; the language is what creates the relations of life.

— Andrei Belyi, The Magic of Words (1910)

At present the formation of new words is a slow process..., and no new words are deliberately coined except as names for material objects. ... [I]t would be quite feasible to invent a vocabulary, perhaps amounting to several thousands of words, which would deal with parts of our experience now practically unamenable to language. ... What is wanted is several thousands of gifted but normal people who would give themselves to word-invention... Given these, I believe we could work wonders with language.

— George Orwell, New Words (1940)

1. Sign Generation and the Internet

There are three types of language activity: *combinative*, *descriptive* and *formative*. Most texts fall under the first type. Everybody combines words some way or another, although the vocabulary and patterns of word combination differ greatly in literary, political, scientific or colloquial language.

The second type includes scholarly works that describe language and define words and the rules of their combination (gram-mar books, dictionaries, etc.).

The third, and the rarest, type introduces new signs into the language (rather than combining or describing those that already exist). We will call it **semiurgy** (Gr *semeion*, sign + *–ourgia*, work; cf. *liturgy, metallurgy*), i.e. sign creation. The word *semiurgy* is itself an example of semiurgy in action. Semiurgy can be defined as efforts to expand and modify the semiosphere.[7]

Word creation may seem an anonymous process taking place at the nation level, yet individual contributions to the vocabulary may be important. Shakespeare alone added about 800 words to English, including *critic, generous, gloomy, hint, luggage, manager,* and *outbreak*.[8] Ben Johnson is credited with *analytic* and *antagonist*.

---

7. Jean Buadrillard (cf. *Systems of objects*, 1968) and the postmodern theory of communi-cation apply the term *semiurgy* to any sign-related activity. I use it narrowly, as the art and practice of creating new signs.

We use many other words with recognized authorships:

> *gas* (a substance), by the Flemish chemist Jan Baptist van Helmont (17th c.)

> *serendipity* (an accidental discovery), by the English writer Horace Walpole (18th c.)

> *psychedelic* (mind-altering drugs), by Humphry Osmond, a British psychiatrist (late 1950s)

> *workaholic* (addicted to work), by Wayne Oates, an American Christian pastor and writer (late 1960s)

> *factoid* (a published alleged fact), by Nor-man Mailer (1973)

> *Newspeak* (a totalitarian language), by George Orwell (1948)

Inventing new words doesn't mean creating Newspeak. Orwell's Newspeak was a way to reduce the vocabulary to a limited num-ber of words laden with ideological attitude. Apart from such political abuse of neolo-gisms, Orwell strongly believed in

---

8. "In all there are 2,035 'first usage' words… assigned to Shakespeare. My estimate is that about 1,700 of these are imaginative coinages on his part. An amaz-ing total, by any standard. And even more amazing is the impact of these words on the subsequent devel-opment of the language. About half of them fell out of use… . But that leaves some 800 clear-cut cases, such as *abstemious*, *accessible*, and *assassination*, which achieved a permanent place in English…" David Crystal. *Words. Words. Words.* Oxford: Oxford Uni-versity Press, 2007, pp. 140–141. Also see Jeffrey McQuain and Stanley Malles. *Coined by Shake-speare: Words & Meanings First Penned by the Bard.* Springfield, MA: Merriam-Webster, 1998

coining new words to express "parts of our experience now practically unamenable to language."

Contrary to the common belief that lan-guage is produced by the entire nation, word coinage is a private enterprise: some-one's mouth utters a new word or a hand writes it down. However, individual contri-butions went unrecorded for millennia, so we can only see the results of centuries of "natural selection" of the vocabulary. Early literary creativity was not individualized, either, as songs and legends were passed down via word of mouth. Literary author-ship came into being with writing.

Nowadays, the information technology spells the end of the folk age of language: the Internet does to language what writing at one point did to literature, i.e., under-mines its folklore nature turning it into an area of individual creativity. Web search capability means that new words will be easier to trace back to their authors, to find out their original meanings and the author's intention: a click on the Search button is all it takes. The Internet also allows circulating a new word to any number of people in a matter of seconds. Neologisms catch on instantly, with their success measured by the number of web pages where they are adopted.

One can anticipate that over time creating new signs will become a booming area of creative work. New, faster data processing technology means accelerated vocabulary replacement to humanize communication. The current explosion of slang and unorthodox spelling on the web points to semiurgy as ever more versatile tool of vocabu-lary innovation.

A century ago, at the dawn of the literary avant-garde, Velimir

Khlebnikov, a Russian futurist poet, prolific wordsmith and language designer, was prophetic about the role of practical "linguistry":

> Making up words is not against the rules of language…
> Just like the man now populates river shallows with
> fish, so linguistry makes it possible to repopulate the
> depleted stream of language with extinct or made-up
> words. We believe they will sparkle with life again, as in
> the first days of creation.[9]

Linguistry, a verbal branch of semiurgy, is to theoretical linguistics what gardening or horticulture is to botany.[10]

Why semiurgy is socially and culturally important? Ludwig Wittgenstein famously said: "The limits of my language mean the limits of my world." Coining new words overcomes these limits and expands our world. It creates not only new signs, but new concepts and ideas, too. Every new word brings about a new meaning, and along with it, a potential for new understanding. Meaning guides human feelings and actions. We ask ourselves, Is it love? Or I'd rather describe the feeling as compassion? friendship? lust? respect? pity? gratitude? Then we act based on which word we've found to describe our feelings best, e.g., get married or divorced, keep dating or break up, etc. The Greek had a number of words for various types and shades of love, such as *eros, mania, philia, agape* – yet in English (and many other European languages, for that matter) there is just one

---

9. Velimir Khlebnikov. *Tvoreniya*. Moscow: Sovetskii pisatel', 1986, p. 627.
10. The term *linguistry* was occasionally used as a synonym of linguistics. I propose using *linguistry* more specifically, as a transformative linguistics, a practical art of cultivating and expanding the lan-guage.

word, *love*, indiscriminately applied to motherland, ice cream, or spouse. New formations derived from the same word through suffixes (cf. *lovedom, lovehood, underloved, dislove, eqiphilia*, etc.) not only add a new layer of meanings to the language, but also new shades to the range of feelings, actions and intentions.

According to Khlebnikov, the word governs the brain, the brain governs the hands, and the hands govern the kingdoms. A mere word can engender new theories and practices, just like a seed, millions of future plants.

My plea to all those who make a living by writing and/or speaking: We all use the bounty of the language as means of our very existence thus profiting from it. We all are language's dependents for life; yet we can repay our debt, at least partially, by enriching language with new words. No law mandates us to contribute a new word per every thousand words used. Let such a payback become a matter of our professional honor.

2. Language Synthesis

Every new discipline or way of thinking, be it quantum physics or Hegel's philosophy, develops its own vocabulary. Quantum me-chanics is impossible without neologisms like *photon*, *quark*, *spin*, *uncertainty principle*, *wave–particle duality*, and so on. From the linguistics standpoint, the devel-opment of every discipline equals the con-tinuous growth of its vocabulary as the system of signs that not only describe the laws of the universe, but also pave the way for new ways of thinking.

Sign creation is especially important in philosophy as it looks for terms/concepts/categories that could free our thinking from the prison of everyday language and common sense preju-dices. Philosophers often fail to find what they need among the existing words and coin new words or assign new meanings to old ones, e.g. *idea* (Plato), *thing-in-itself* (Kant), *Aufhebung* (Hegel), *Übermensch* (Nietzsche), and *Zeitigung* (Heidegger). Their language is rich in neologisms referring to their most fundamental con-cepts that did not fit into the existing vocabulary. Philosophy creates new terms and meanings just like economy creates new goods and values.

During the 20th century, the Anglo-American philosophy was dominated by the linguistic-analytic approach with its emphasis on logical clarity and the analysis of everyday, scientific, and philosophical language (reducing it to the "atoms" of mean-ing) as philosophy's primary task. At the same time, the synthetic aspect of language and the task of producing new terms and concepts were all but ignored.

Philosophy of *language synthesis*, heralded by G. Deleuze and F. Guattari (*A Thousand Plateaus*, 1987; *What is Philosophy?* 1996), may be seen as a new alternative to the tradition of language analysis. To the extent that the subject of philosophy are language-based ideas and universals, the task of philosophy is to expand our mental vocabulary and grammar, to generate new words, concepts, lexical and semantic fields, and syntax. Thus philosophy helps the mankind expand the scope of the speakable, conceivable and thinkable, and, therefore, of do-able and feasible.

This postanalytic approach would focus on the synthesis of new terms, concepts, and statements based on their analysis. Every analytic act provides an opportunity for a new synthesis. Breaking down a statement allows to recombine the elements and create new statements, thus opening new areas for thought and speech.

If we apply the approach of George Moore (a founder of analytic philosophy) to the statement "stupidity is a vice," this statement would be equivalent to "I have a negative attitude towards stupidity," or "Stupidity creates negative emotions in me." These statements tell nothing new, they just clarify what the original one means. The creative, synthetically oriented approach to this statement, however, uses it as a potential foundation for other, alternative and more informative, "wondrous" statements (Aristotle said that philosophy is born out of the feeling of wonder). Analysis itself is pointless unless it leads to a new synthesis.

Let's suggest a series of questions and alternative propositions to the same analytically trivial statement. Is stupidity always a vice, or in certain cases can be considered a virtue? If wit can be applied to justify a vice, then can stupidity serve as manifesta-tion of innocence? If stupidity is sometimes used as a means to a virtuous goal, can it then be considered a virtue itself? A Russian satirist of the 19th c., M. Saltykov-Shchedrin, coined a term that has come into common usage: *blagoglupost*, best rendered by the English neologism **virtupidity** – something stupid but well-meant, a sublime nonsense, a pompous triviality.

Now, if stupidity, in a sense, can be a virtue, then malice may be virtuous as well, or, rather, virtuousness may be mean. If so, we could call the well-intentioned malice **benemalence** (cf. *benevolence*), of which Dostoevsky's Great Inquisitor is an example: people can do horrible things with the best of intentions. The Bolshevik Revolution had as one of its slogans "Let us drive humankind to happiness with an iron hand," which is another instance of **benemalence**.

So analyzing a trivial statement may lead to a synthesis of non-trivial, thought-provoking statements and new words. Such an operation can be formalized by the symbol ÷ as the sign of logical bifurcation (i.e., an alternative emerging from a statement analysis). The elements of the statement which precede the sign ÷ are variables, whereas their alternatives/variations that follow are new statements condensed into new terms:

Stupidity ÷ is a vice.

Stupidity can be ÷ a vice (but may not be).

Stupidity can be ÷ a virtue (under certain circumstances).

Good intention is a premise of virtue.

Stupidity can be a vehicle of good intentions. – **Virtupidity**

Malice can be a vehicle of good intentions. – **Benemalence**

Analysis and synthesis feed and inform each other. Every analysis that isolates elements of a word/concept can lead to synthesis, i.e., recombination of these elements into other words, concepts, new terms, statements, disciplines, methods, and worldviews. The level of synthesis depends on the level of the underlying analysis. Accordingly, analytic philosophy can be interpreted and revised in terms of synthesis.

3. Magic, Logic and Aesthetics of the Word:
Dictionary Entry as a Genre

Any verbal sign, in addition to phonemes and morphemes, includes a referent, or a signified, described by its dictionary definition, as well as its actual and potential uses (the pragmatic sphere, according to the Wittgenstein's view that the meaning of a word is its use in speech). Thus, to fully introduce a new verbal sign we need a dictionary entry which would include the word with its definition and samples of usage.

Dictionary entry is an important form of semiotic discourse that comprehensively describes a verbal sign as a unity of the signifier, the signified, and the context/usage. It is also a **semiurgic** genre. The dictionary entry has been barely subject to linguistic study.[11] There is, though, a short article titled "The Paradox of a Dictionary Entry" by Natalia Shvedova,[12] an outstanding Russian linguist. The paper has no reference section, since there is no "prior art." According to Shvedova, the "dictionary entry is a linguistic genre that tells not only about the

---

11. Sidney I. Landau provides a study of the dictionary work in *Dictionaries: The Art and Craft of Lexi-cography* (1989); Chapter 3 (pp. 76–119) is the most relevant to our discussion. The book is a helpful survey but does not elaborate on the dictionary entry as a linguistic genre of its own. David Crystal (*op.cit.*, pp. 33–39) provides a good introduction into the work of a lexicographer.
12. Natal'ia Yu. Shvedova. *Russkii iazyk. Izbrannye raboty* (Russian Language: Selected Works). Mos-cow: Iazyki Slavianskoi Kul'tury, 2005, p. 420.

word itself, but also about its various linguistic environments: contextual, classificational, derivational, phraseological, and functional." Shvedova sees the dictionary entry as a model of the entire language universe: "The macroworld of language appears through the microworld of a word, as if concentrated in it. A word as a unit of language represents the entire language…"

The dictionary entry may be a complex piece indeed, with various grammatical and stylistic markers, etymological/historical references, etc., but three elements are crucial: (i) the headword itself; (ii) the definition; and (iii) phrases that show how the word is used in typical contexts. Here are two examples, one from a conventional dictionary, another from my *PreDictionary*:

> **happiness**, *n*. [from *happy*] – good luck; good fortune; prosperity; a state of well-being; a pleasurable or enjoyable experience.

> All happiness bechance to thee in Milan! – W. Shakespeare. I had the happiness of seeing you. – W.S. Gilbert

> **happicle** *n* (*happy* + suffix *-icle*, as in *particle*, *icicle*) — a single happy occurrence or a momentary feeling of happiness, a particle of happiness.

> **Happicles** make life worth living, even a not too happy one.

> There is no happiness in this world, but there are **happicles**. Sometimes we can catch them, fleeting and unpredictable as they are.

Semiotics embraces three dimensions of a sign and has three

branches, accordingly: (i) the syntactics that describes the elements (phonetic, morphological, lexical) of a sign or a sign sequence and relationships between them; (ii) the semantics that de-scribes the meaning (any concepts/objects to which the sign refers); and (iii) pragmatics dealing with the sign's uses and communicative functions.

The dictionary entry covers all these aspects: the headword represents a syntactical unit (a set of morphemes and phonemes); the definition, the semantics (describes the sign's meaning); the examples reflect the pragmatics by showing situations/contexts where the sign would be appropriate and typically used.

Thus, the dictionary entry comprehensively reproduces a semi-urgic act with its syntactic, semantic and pragmatic dimensions. Creating a new sign/word takes much more than just combining phonemes and morphemes in a way never used before; it would also require explaining its meaning and providing potential context(s) of its usage. Designing entries that introduce new words rather than deal with existing ones, goes beyond a purely academic pursuit. In fact, this applies to any dictionary. "A good dictionary thrives on the brilliance of its definitions. They have to be clear, succinct, relevant, and discriminating. They can also be elegant, humorous, quirky, and memorable. Definitions… involve imagination and creativity, just as any other literary genre."[13] A projective dictionary should be especially ingenious and creative, a "linguo-fantasy," a "lexi-fiction."

In a traditional dictionary designed to clarify words found in

---

13. David Crystal, *op. cit.*, p. 33.

texts, the reference system can be described as text—dictionary—text: we encounter a word, look for its definition in the dictionary, then go back to the text. Projective dictionaries can't refer to any actual text since the words have never been used before. New words relate to the language as a system, so the reference pattern would be (pre)dictionary—language—possible text (one that could include a new word taken from that projective dictionary).

For example, the word *conaster* refers to the English lexicon (rather than any existing text), specifically, to those words derived from the Latin *aster* (star), especially to the motivating word *disaster* (literally, "away from stars"). Of course, any examples used in projective dictionaries would be made up by the author, since there is no existing text to quote.

> **conaster** *n* (Lat *cum*, with + Gr *astron*, star) — literally *with star*, the antonym to *disaster* (literally "away from stars"); the fortunate outcome of an imminent disaster; the sensation of a dodged catastrophe remembered from the vantage point of safety.
>
> There were several **conasters** in my life that I can only attribute to God's undeserved mercy.
>
> You were born under a lucky star. This **conaster** was an amazing mix of chance and miracle.

Semiurgy is a holistic act that integrates the magic, science and art of sign creation. A semiurgic act limited to the syntactics alone (i.e. combining phonemes and morphemes into a signifier) would result in magic spells, incantation, glossolalia, speaking in tongues, often as part of mystical or religious practice. For example, reciting an unintelligible mantra would plunge the believer into an ecstatic or meditative state. What is meaningless for some may be a holy language for others.

A semiurgic act limited to the semantics alone (i.e. generating concepts/ideas) would fall into the area of intellectual, philosophical or scientific creativity.

A semiurgic act limited to the pragmatics alone would be verbal art, such as poetry or prose, i.e. the art of combining words the best possible way to produce the most expressive and beautiful speech. But in a true semiurgic act all of these aspects come together to make up the microcosm of the dictionary entry: the newly crafted word is the magical element; the definition is the scientific/logical component; and the example is the artistic/aesthetic component. Thus, what we call the dictionary entry is, in fact, the miniature manifestation of the entire semiosphere.

The word magic usually needs no clarity or defined meaning; in fact, the incoherence may even contribute to a mantra's effect. Similarly, verbalizing scientific concepts may not require artistic expression. Used separately, the three kinds of semiotic activity may interfere with one another and the intended goal — the magic of the word, the scientific accuracy of the concept, and the artistry of speech. But only a semiurgic act combining sound, meaning, and usage would be a comprehensive manifestation of the semiosphere.

Three identities coexist in a semiurg: a magician conjuring up a new word from the depths of a language; a scholar carefully defining the word to bring it to its unique place in the vocabulary; and a writer plotting a situation that would require the new word.

The process of sign creation can start anywhere and proceed in any direction, not necessarily following the 'word–meaning–usage' path. For example, a situation or a concept may emerge and call for a new word. But as soon as one of the semiurg's three identities have initiated the process, the other two have to be involved: the magician would ask the scholar for a definition, and the writer for a plausible context. Or the scholar may order a word for a new concept from the magician, and a convincing usage sample from the writer. The three elements are inseparable in any dictionary entry, which, for this very reason, is the most comprehensive verbal genre that unites the magic, logic and aesthetics of the word.

Atelos was founded in 1995 as a project of Hip's Road and is devoted to publishing, under the sign of poetry, writing that challenges conventional, limiting definitions of poetry.

All the works published as part of the Atelos project are comissioned specifically for it, and each is involved in some way with crossing traditional genre boundaries, including, for example, those that would separate theory from practice, poetry from prose, essay from drama, the visual image from the verbal, the literary from the nonliterary, and so forth.

The Atelos project when complete will consist of 50 volumes.

The project directors and editors are Lyn Hejinian and Travis Ortiz. The director for text production and design is Travis Ortiz; the director for cover production and design is Ree Katrak.

Atelos (current volumes):

1. *The Literal World*, by Jean Day
2. *Bad History*, by Barrett Watten
3. *True*, by Rae Armantrout
4. *Pamela: A Novel*, by Pamela Lu
5. *Cable Factory 20*, by Lytle Shaw
6. *R-hu* by Leslie Scalapino

Distributed by:

Small Press Distribution
1341 Seventh Street
Berkeley, California
      94710-1403

Atelos
P O Box 5814
Berkeley, California
      94705-0814

to order from SPD call 510-524-1668 or toll-free 800-869-7553
fax orders to: 510-524-0852
orders via email at: orders@spdbooks.org
orders online from: www.spdbooks.org

PreDictionary
was printed in an edition of 750 copies
at Thomson-Shore, Inc.
Text design by Shelby Rachleff
using Garamond for the text, Modern No. 20 and Didot
for the titles, and Georgia for the page numbers.
Cover design by Shelby Rachleff.